# EXPERIENCES OF THE PARANORMAL

## REAL CONVERSATIONS WITH DEMONS

Terry Fox

Daniel Gomez Enterprises, L.L.C.

*Real Conversations with Demons: Experiences of the Paranormal*
Written by Terry Fox

Published by Daniel Gomez Enterprises LLC /February 2025
Contact Info: (210) 663-5954 / Email: Info@DanielGomezGlobal.com ISBN:

# Dedication

I would like to dedicate this book to my mom, Norma Faye Oliver, who gave me prayer and enormous support on this project.

# Table of Contents

# Introduction

Fellow seekers of truth and warriors in the battle,

Have you ever felt like life is a battlefield, with unseen forces working against you? You're not alone. Welcome to this journey of discovery, where we'll dive into the realm of paranormal and spiritual warfare, armed with knowledge and the power of faith.

This book is not your typical everyday read, and it's certainly not your typical conversation starter. Oftentimes, people are afraid to express their thoughts and their paranormal experiences. This book will illuminate the reality of Satanists, witchcraft, and other aspects of the occult. This book will help you to be prepared to face head-on the battles that happen beyond what your eyes can see.

Why? Because understanding the work of Satan and his demons isn't about entertaining some wild fantasy or just a hobby. It's about equipping ourselves with the tools and knowledge to navigate the challenges the enemy throws at us. It's about being aware that our struggles are not always just happenstance but could be a result of evil forces beyond the physical realm.

Now, before you think we're delving into some dark and eerie territory, take a deep breath. Spiritual warfare and the paranormal world are not about fear mongering; it's about embracing the power of love, faith, and applying authority over darkness.

We'll explore the concepts of spiritual attacks, the tactics of the enemy, and how we can armor up with divine wisdom and strength. The goal isn't to create paranoia or superstition, but to provide knowledge that will empower you to discern and resist the negative influences that seek to hinder your purpose and destroy you.

Let's make it clear: we are all in a spiritual battle, whether we know it or not. You cannot win a war without knowledge of your enemy. We welcome all curious hearts, regardless of your faith background. This book is here to offer insights, inspire courage, and ignite your spiritual journey.

Expect stories of triumph over adversity, practical tips for self-protection, and reflections that will challenge your perspective about deliverance, exorcisms, and demonic strongholds. You will read about many of our paranormal cases and the conversations that we have had with demons. Together, we'll investigate the field of the paranormal and uncover the ways in which spiritual forces impact our lives.

So, fasten your seatbelt and prepare to explore the realms of spiritual warfare like never before. Remember, we're in this together. Our goal is to make you more aware of the spirit world. You'll emerge with a stronger heart, a clearer mind, and a renewed sense of purpose.

Thanks for taking time to read this work. I hope you will share these truths with others. Let's journey on.

Blessings, Paranormal Pastor

Terry Fox

*Chapter 1*

# The Dark Side of the Paranormal

This story begins while I was serving as a pastor as well as a reserve lieutenant with the Nueces County Sheriff's Office in Corpus Christi, Texas. I was a fairly young pastor, and I was very busy at that time in my life. I always had a desire to help in law enforcement, even though I was actively serving as lead pastor at Gardendale Baptist Church. It was one of the largest Baptist churches in South Texas at the time. I made a lot of time available in my schedule to help with the sheriff's office.

One day, I was assigned to a case in missing persons, which was a division of the sheriff's office. We were asked to help find two runaway girls that had been reported missing several months apart. We discovered the whereabouts of one of the girls and apprehended her. During my investigation, I was stunned that she revealed to me her reason for running away from home. She told us an unbelievable story. It is a story I could hardly wrap my mind around. This case opened my eyes to the fact that there is a very dark side to the paranormal. It became reality to me and the other officers as we worked on this case together.

This juvenile girl was running away from home for good reason. Her family was involved in a satanic cult. Part of being in that cult was that they would make themselves available to the other members sexually. She was approximately 17 years of age and just about to turn 18. She did not want to go home. She was terrified because her parents were involved in the cult, and she knew they would punish her for trying to escape from the home and the Satanic cult.

Her family was connected to ruthless people that were part of evil satanic rituals involving human sacrifices. She had been ordered to have sex with both male and female members of the cult. When she became pregnant, they kept her until after the birth of the baby. She was supervised by a midwife that was assigned to her. Shortly after the baby was born, the girl was forced to participate in a ritual to sacrifice her baby to Satan. She was told that if she ever told anyone, she would be sent to jail herself because of her involvement.

On one occasion, I took this girl to a diner to feed her and to hear more about her story. While there, she looked out the window and recognized a vehicle of one of the cult members. She became very fearful that they were going to hurt us. I assured her that she was safe with me. She said a demon was assigned to watch her and would know everything we said and did.

A few months later, we found another girl who was a little bit younger than the first. As we spent time interviewing her, I understood why she was running from home and not attending school. She had been a victim of the same Satanic cult. Each girl shared their stories separately, which confirmed the validity of their experiences. These girls did not know each other and had no opportunity to corroborate their stories. Both girls shared that they were being used sexually and abused in other areas. Both girls reported to me that the satanic leader had assigned a particular demon to them and that the demon would report it to the people in the cult if they disobeyed the rules.

We also found out the girls had been threatened and were told that if they tried to escape or go to law enforcement, their lives would be ended. Both girls became pregnant at different times but in similar situations. They had both been impregnated at satanic meetings where sexual orgies occurred on a regular basis. They both were used for sex by cult members. Both girls shared that they had been assigned a midwife, and they were not assigned to any doctor. The midwife who was connected to the Satanic cult was responsible for making sure they had their babies. According to their testimony, both girls had their babies, although without hospital records this could not be verified. We have discovered that in some of these satanic cults, this is a very common practice. The reason for having these children was so that could be used for a human sacrifice. Both girls gave testimony that after they had the babies, the babies were sacrificed.

As we investigated, we found out that this was indeed a true satanic cult. They had connections, not only in South Texas but in Mexico. In our research, we started running different names that were involved. We discovered many different aliases being used. They also had connections in Chicago, Illinois. Each girl shared very traumatic testimonies, and it was extremely hard to listen to them tell how they had been mistreated. As a police officer, it was very difficult.

I remember when the first girl told me that they had used her baby as a human sacrifice. It was a difficult story to believe, but I could tell that she was terrified, and I sensed that she was telling the truth.

When I heard the story of the second girl, I was appalled that human sacrifice was happening in Texas. I started receiving death threats from my involvement in this case. One death threat came through the sheriff's office, and others came to our home. We started getting phone calls, and I was being warned to get out of this case and to drop it. I discovered that federal agents were assigned to this case and other similar cases. We also discovered the people in the cult were not only into Satanism but into a lot of other illegal activity. I was able to trace some of the main players and discovered that they were connected to even larger crime rings in Chicago. They were involved in drugs, human trafficking, and money laundering.

Sometimes criminals make a covenant with Satan and demons so that they will be protected by them.

The May 16, 1985 episode of 20/20 exposed the fact that Satanism was active in the United States. This episode can be found at https://www.youtube.com/watch?v=9GudmlgTfOE (20/20 (May 16, 1985) Satanists, Bogdanovich vs Hefner)

They interviewed police officers about satanic crimes, including murder. They also interview Mike Warnke, a former Satanist priest. They report about many incidents of animal sacrifices and evidence of rituals in every state. This episode of 20/20 opened the eyes of many people in America to the truth that Satanism is a concern for this country. The dark side of the paranormal was exposed as never before.

These experiences opened my eyes to the reality of the dark side of the paranormal world. I began to research spiritual warfare and Satanism. I put together a conference called "Satanism in America" and did presentations across the country. I shared these experiences at many churches, Bible conferences, and even at police academies.

8:21 / 49:18

*Chapter 2*

# Satan Has Lied to Us: Biblical Perspective

Satan has lied to many people. He has caused many people to question his existence. Many people underestimate his passion and do not realize his purpose. Remember, Satan is not a true friend to anyone. By the way, even the demons don't like Satan and are afraid of him. Satan hates everything that God has made, but he especially hates God's special creation, which is humanity. We have been warned about Satan in the scriptures. John 8:44 says that Satan is a liar. It says, "Ye are of your father the devil, and the lusts of your father ye will do. He was a murderer from the beginning, and abode not in the truth, because there is no truth in him. When he speaketh a lie, he speaketh of his own: for he is a liar, and the father of it." (KJV) The number one lie of the devil is that he is not real or that he is just a joke. Many people picture him as a red cartoon character with a pitchfork and a long tail. Unfortunately, they have no idea who they are dealing with. Let me be clear here. Satan has lied to us!

I will be sharing with you some personal experiences of the four hundred cases that I have dealt with. Many pastors and seminaries teach very little about the paranormal. They have done their best to either ignore or discredit the truth about the reality of spiritual warfare and paranormal activity in today's world. They will argue that this subject is not biblical or necessary for today. I have learned that Satan and his demons do not want to be exposed, and I believe that there is a strong movement from the dark side to try and keep pastors from being involved in the paranormal and deliverance ministry. Many pastors and ministers may not get involved in paranormal work because of fear.

I feel indebted to three pastors and mentors that have helped to shape and have impacted my life in this paranormal ministry. One of those was Dr. Sam Cathey. Dr. Cathey was originally from Arkansas and preached many thousands of times all over the world in Baptist churches and was known as a demonologist. He has written books about demons and the reality of demons. When I was a young pastor, Sam Cathey said I needed to understand the teaching of demons because they are attacking people, they're attacking church members, and they're attacking non-Christians. He said it's going to get worse and it's going to get darker. Dr. Cathey is now in heaven, but I know that he would approve of this ministry.

Dr. Stan Coffey was a dynamic pastor in Amarillo, Texas, and Albuquerque, New Mexico. I preached for him on several occasions when he was a mega pastor. He was a well-known leader in the Southern Baptist convention for many years. Many times, Dr. Coffey said to me, "We're going to have to get more involved in battling these demons that are obviously attacking and hurting people." Dr. Bill Bennett also influenced me greatly. He was my pastor at First Baptist Church in Fort Smith, Arkansas. He was a renowned theologian and author and known as a successful pastor all over the world. He stressed to me that we need to do a better job in our churches about teaching the truth about spiritual warfare. I had the privilege of serving three years on his staff as personal assistant to this great man of God.

Sometimes you will hear people say, "I don't believe in something, so therefore it's not true." They will tell you, "I'm not going to believe in anything that I cannot smell, see, or touch." However, you are going to limit yourself if that's the standard you use. You would never see a bullet coming at you, but you're sure to know when it hits you. We don't see the wind blowing, but we feel its effects. Many people say they believe in Jesus, but they have never seen him. When it comes to the study and the work of the paranormal, I believe it's important that we establish a biblical worldview.

For many years, pastors have told their congregations that if they just keep their focus on Jesus, they don't have to worry about evil coming after them. This is not true or scriptural! Unfortunately, in many cases, the devil and his army of demons will go after God's most faithful people! An example from the Bible is Job. Satan noticed the righteousness of Job and wanted to kill him! In John 10:10, Jesus says, "A thief does not come except to steal, and to kill, and to destroy. I have come that they may have life and have it more abundantly." I personally would like to make the case that the more you are trying to live for Jesus and to serve the Lord, the greater the possibility of spiritual warfare coming against you.

According to the Merriam-Webster dictionary, the word paranormal is defined as "scientifically unexplainable, supernatural." In the context of this book, I will be showing you the reality of many concepts concerning supernatural activity in the lives of many people. I will be revealing truths about the unseen spiritual world. I have discovered in life that there are many factual experiences that cannot be explained by science or human reasoning. Based on my forty years of ministry as a Southern Baptist pastor and a decade of serving in law enforcement, I will be sharing real paranormal cases from a biblical worldview.

Most mainline denominations, evangelical pastors and theologians have avoided this subject altogether. Many seminaries and Bible colleges teach very little about it. They have done their best to either ignore or discredit the truth about the reality of spiritual warfare and paranormal activity in today's world. They will argue that this subject is not biblical or necessary for today. They want to say that people are suffering from paranoia or mental illness only. They would say that even though there are anecdotes in the bible of paranormal experiences, such as demons attacking individuals, and the casting out of demons by Jesus, his disciples, and the early church, it is no longer relevant for our culture today. I believe their position defies the true teaching found in the scriptures. I am convinced their point of view and philosophy on this subject is not only incorrect but has left many people unprepared and defenseless. If you think this is not true, try to go find help from pastors or churches to get rid of the attacks from the devil and his demons. In my opinion, this is a shame because the church should be willing and available to help people in their time of darkest need.

Most people probably realize that there are people in their lives that do not like them. Whether people realize it or not, we all have three enemies. The Bible teaches us that we all have three enemies.

## I. Self - the Flesh:

Romans 13:14 says, "But put on the Lord Jesus Christ, and make no provision for the flesh, to fulfill its lusts."

Some examples of the flesh could be selfishness, rebellion, or any temptation for unhealthy addictions that hurt us. Dr. Sam Cathey says,

"Whatever you do of a selfish nature is an open door for demons to begin to draw you away from God's will for your life. You can depend on them to come through that open door! Close that door! Because sin not dealt with allows the demons to build a stronghold. If you think strongholds can't come in the life of a Christian, why did

Paul tell believers in II Corinthians 10 that 'Our weapons are not carnal but spiritual and mighty unto God to the pulling down of strongholds'?

How do strongholds come into the life of a Christian? We get selfish; we disobey God; we go into a spirit of rebellion, living our own lives. Demons then move in and start influencing our environment and our thinking because we are walking in the flesh and a stronghold is built. It just keeps getting stronger and stronger! That's why some cannot control their moods. That's why some can't get rid of their dirty habits. That's why some cannot change their attitude. That's why some can't get control over certain habits in life. It is because there is a demonic stronghold there." (Quote from Spiritual Warfare by Dr. Sam Cathey, p. 20, Golden Rule Book Press, Inc., Orlando, FL, 1987)

I want to point out that even though some of our struggles begin as a struggle from our own flesh, they can open the door for a demonic attachment. These strongholds can be very difficult to overcome.

## II. Society - the World:

I John 2:15 says, "Do not love the world or the things in the world. If anyone loves the world, the love of the Father is not in him."

Peer pressure from people in the world can cause us to have wrong priorities or to do bad things. Teachings or beliefs that divert our attention from God are from the world. We should be watchful not to be influenced by social media, Hollywood, astrology, or Zodiac signs. We should not listen to advice from fortune tellers or mediums. Even the busyness of the world can influence us and distract us from doing more important things that really matter!

## III. Satan - the Devil:

1 Peter 5:8 says, "Be sober, be vigilant; because your adversary the devil walks about like a roaring lion, seeking whom he may devour."

Ephesians 6:12 says, "For we do not wrestle against flesh and blood, but against principalities, against powers, against the rulers of the darkness of this age, against spiritual hosts of wickedness in the heavenly places."

An example of this would be that Satan wants to control us and destroy our lives. As you will continue in the book, you will come to understand these concepts in more depth.

## Where did Satan and the demons come from, and what will happen to them in the end?

Revelation 12:7-9 says, "And war broke out in heaven: Michael and his angels fought with the dragon; and the dragon and his angels fought, but they did not prevail, nor was a place found for them in heaven any longer. So the great dragon was cast out, that serpent of old, called the Devil and Satan, who deceives the whole world; he was cast to the earth, and his angels were cast out with him."

The Bible is very clear on this subject. It tells us that there was a fight in the heavens between good and evil. The devil (called a great dragon) and one-third of the angels rebelled against God and tried to take over heaven, but they failed. These rebellious angels were thrown down to the earth. These fallen angels became the demonic entities that we are still fighting today. The Bible clearly teaches that at the end of time, the devil and all his demons will be judged by God and cast into the lake of fire, where they will remain forever. But until then, we must be prepared to battle these dark forces skillfully and strategically.

Revelation 20:10 says, "The devil, who deceived them, was cast into the lake of fire and brimstone where the beast and the false prophet are. And they will be tormented day and night forever and ever."

Nearly all religions in the world teach that there is a battle between good and evil. Even in modern-day movies and television, it is a common theme that in the battle between good and evil, the good side will win. There is always a villain, and in real life, the villain is the devil and his demons.

I want to share with you some examples from the Bible to clarify that demons are real. They are unclean spirits, and they can be cast out. On many occasions, my team and I have discussed that dealing with them makes us feel dirty and exhausted. I frequently refer to the demons as "dirty demons."

## Jesus Cast Out an Unclean Spirit in Capernaum

Mark 1:23-27 says, "Now there was a man in their synagogue with an unclean spirit. And he cried out, saying, 'Let us alone! What have we to do with You, Jesus of Nazareth? Did You come to destroy us? I know who You are—the Holy One of God!' But Jesus rebuked him, saying, 'Be quiet, and come out of him!' And when the unclean spirit had convulsed him and cried out with a loud voice, he came out of him. Then they were all amazed, so that they questioned among themselves, saying, 'What is this? What new doctrine is this? For with authority, He commands even the unclean spirits, and they obey Him.'"

This person was in the synagogue in Capernaum. Luke 4:33–37 also records this event. The demons wanted to be left alone. They knew who Jesus was and from where he came. They knew Jesus could destroy them. A person can have more than one unclean spirit at a time. They can act or speak as a group or as individuals. Jesus rebuked him, saying, "Be quiet, and come out of him!" Unclean spirits often try to hurt their hosts. Jesus has authority over the unclean spirits, and they obey him.

## The Daughter with a Demon

Mark 7:25-30 says, "For a woman whose young daughter had an unclean spirit heard about Him, and she came and fell at His feet. The woman was a Greek, a Syro-Phoenician by birth, and she kept asking Him to cast the demon out of her daughter. But Jesus said to her, 'Let the children be filled first, for it is not good to take the children's bread and throw it to the little dogs.' And she answered and said to Him, 'Yes, Lord, yet even the little dogs under the table eat from the children's crumbs.' Then He said to her, 'For this saying go your way; the demon has gone out of your daughter." And when she had come to her house, she found the demon gone out, and her daughter lying on the bed."

The devil is not a fair fighter. He does not leave children or women alone. This woman called on Jesus to cast the demon out of her daughter. As parents, we have the right and authority to help our children as well. Jesus was not even in the same house, but when He spoke, the girl was made whole, and the devil was gone out of the daughter at that moment. Warfare praying is good even from a distance. This event is also mentioned in Matthew 15:22–28.

Prayer and Fasting May be Needed to Successfully Cast Out a Demon Mark 9:17–29 says, "Then one of the crowd answered and said, 'Teacher, I brought You my son, who has a mute spirit. And wherever it seizes him, it throws him down; he foams at the mouth, gnashes his teeth, and becomes rigid. So I spoke to Your disciples, that they should cast it out, but they could not.' He answered him and said, 'O faithless generation, how long shall I be with you? How long shall I bear with you? Bring him to Me.' Then they brought him to Him. And when he saw Him, immediately the spirit convulsed him, and he fell on the ground and wallowed, foaming at the mouth. So, he asked his father, 'How long has this been happening to him?' And he said, 'From childhood. And often he has thrown him both into the fire and into the water to destroy him. But if You can do anything, have compassion on us and help us.' Jesus said to him, 'If you can believe, all things are possible to him who believes.' Immediately the father of the child cried out and said with tears, 'Lord, I believe; help my unbelief!' When Jesus saw that the people came running together, He rebuked the unclean spirit, saying to it, 'Deaf and dumb spirit, I command you, come out of him and enter him no more!' Then the spirit cried out, convulsed him greatly, and came out of him. And he became one dead, so that many said, 'He is dead.' But Jesus took him by the hand and lifted him up, and he arose. And when He had come into the house, His disciples asked Him privately, 'Why could we not cast it out?' So He said to them, "This kind can come out by nothing but prayer and fasting."

A spirit can enter into a child. A spirit can cause someone to be deaf and dumb and to hurt themselves. A spirit can cause someone to be a lunatic, as the Matthew version relays. A spirit will often try to cause its host to kill himself. A spirit can stay a long time. Some spirits will not come out without much prayer and fasting. When the father of this child believed and cried out, "Lord, I believe; help my unbelief!" Jesus charged the spirit to "come out of him and enter him no more." We can ask Jesus to do the same thing for us. We can ask him to help our unbelief. Then, when we have prayed and fasted, we can charge a spirit to come out and enter no more. Note that evil spirits can come and go. It is important to tell them not to come back! Also see Matthew 17:14-21 and Luke 9:38-42.

The Matthew version includes a famous quote. Matthew 17:19-21

says, "Then the disciples came to Jesus privately and said, 'Why could we not cast it out?' So, Jesus said to them, 'Because of your unbelief; for assuredly, I say to you, if you have faith as a mustard seed, you will say to this mountain, 'Move from here to there,' and it will move; and nothing will be impossible for you. However, this kind does not go out except by prayer and fasting.'"

The disciples could not cast out this kind of demon because of their unbelief. It takes at least more faith than the disciples had at this point to cast this kind of spirit out. We must have faith. It is only through the authority given to us by Jesus and the power of the Holy Spirit that we can be successful in a battle against evil. Jesus tells us to be the light of the world in Matthew 5:14. If we have a relationship with Jesus and embrace our role as the light of the world, we can overcome darkness. Nothing shall be impossible to us! The following verse reminds us that there are different kinds of evil spirits. Some are more powerful than others. Remember the words found in

Ephesians 6:12. "For we do not wrestle against flesh and blood, but against principalities, against powers, against the rulers of the darkness of this age, against spiritual hosts of wickedness in the heavenly places."

I John 3:8 says, "He who sins is of the devil, for the devil has sinned from the beginning. For this purpose, the Son of God was manifested, that He might destroy the works of the devil."

We must remember that in battling the works of the devil, we can triumph! I am always excited to share with people that the Mighty Spirit, which is the Holy Spirit, has more power than any evil spirit.

## Our Involvement Today in the Fight Between Good and Evil

First of all, let me say how thankful I am for those in the past, like Jesus and his disciples, as seen in the previous examples. They showed us their willingness to engage the dark forces that were attacking people. The Bible gives these and many other examples for us to follow and from which we can glean information and inspiration.

As believers, we are told by Jesus in Matthew 5:14, "Ye are the light of the world." Light can overpower the darkness.

Mark 16:17a says, "And these signs will follow those who believe: In My name they will cast out demons."

In John 14:12, Jesus makes an amazing statement. He says, "Most assuredly, I say to you, he who believes in Me, the works that I do he will do also; and greater works than these he will do, because I go to My Father."

These verses clearly teach that just as Jesus and his disciples cast out demons, we also have been given the authority through the power of the Holy Spirit to cast out demons.

As believers, it is important for us to be reminded of our position and power in Christ and to use God's authority that has been given to us. We can be conquerors over the darkness.

I John 4:4 says, "You are of God, little children, and have overcome them, because He who is in you is greater than he who is in the world."

Romans 8:37–39 says, "Yet in all these things we are more than conquerors through Him who loved us. For I am persuaded that neither death nor life, nor angels nor principalities nor powers, nor things present nor things to come, nor height nor depth, nor any other created thing, shall be able to separate us from the love of God, which is in Christ Jesus our Lord."

Philippians 4:13 says, "I can do all things through Christ who strengthens me."

Reasons believers should be involved in helping people be set free from darkness:

1. As believers, we are following the example of Jesus. I John 3:8 says, "He who sins is of the devil, for the devil has sinned from the beginning. For this purpose, the Son of God was manifested, that He might destroy the works of the devil." Fighting darkness was a priority for Jesus.

2. The Bible gives us instructions on how to fight the devil and his demons. Ephesians 6:10–18 says, "Finally, my brethren, be strong in the Lord and in the power of His might. Put on the whole armor of God, that you may be able to stand against the wiles of the devil. For we do not wrestle against flesh and blood, but against principalities, against powers, against the rulers of the darkness of this age, against spiritual hosts of wickedness in the heavenly places. Therefore, take up the whole armor of God, that you may be able to withstand in the evil day, and having done all, to stand. Stand therefore, having girded your waist with truth, having put on the breastplate of righteousness, and having shod your feet with the preparation of the gospel of peace; above all, taking the shield of faith with which you will be able to quench all the fiery darts of the wicked one. And take the helmet of salvation and the sword of the Spirit, which is the word of God; praying always with all prayer and supplication in the Spirit, being watchful to this end with all perseverance and supplication for all the saints—"

3. People are desperate and pleading for help, so it pleases God when we assist them. Like the disciples of Jesus' day, we can help people have victory over demonic forces. Luke 9:1-2 says, "Then He called His twelve disciples together and gave them power and authority over all demons, and to cure diseases. He sent them to preach the kingdom of God and to heal the sick." This demonstrates that we, as disciples, have been given authority to cast out demons.

Luke 10:17 points out that the authority to cast out demons was not just limited to Jesus and his twelve disciples. It says, "The seventy-two returned with joy, saying, 'Lord, even the demons submit to us in your name." Acts 16:18 shows Paul casting a demon out of a girl who was a fortune teller. He said, "I command you in the name of Jesus Christ to come out of her! And it came out right away. We can cast out demons with the authority given to us by Jesus. I John 4:4 reminds us that "greater is he that is in you, than he that is in the world."

4. People are blessed when they see the power of God defeat the devil. Luke 8:38-39 says, "Now the man from whom the demons had departed begged Him that he might be with Him. But Jesus sent him away, saying, "Return to your own house and tell what great things God has done for you." And he went his way and proclaimed throughout the whole city what great things Jesus had done for him."

5. When Satan and his demons are defeated, it opens the door for people to connect with God. 2 Corinthians 4:3-6 says, "But even if our gospel is veiled, it is veiled to those who are perishing, whose minds the god of this age has blinded, who do not believe, lest the light of the gospel of the glory of Christ, who is the image of God, should shine on them. For we do not preach ourselves, but Christ Jesus the Lord, and

ourselves your bondservants for Jesus' sake. For it is the God who commanded light to shine out of darkness, who has shone in our hearts to give the light of the knowledge of the glory of God in the face of Jesus Christ." We are to be the light of the world to dispel the darkness. One of the greatest joys of doing this ministry is helping people enter into a personal relationship with Jesus.

Before I conclude this chapter, I would like to remind you of three truths about the paranormal. The reality of the paranormal (Ephesians 6:10 – 12) is taught in the scriptures. We have seen in this chapter that demons, also called unclean spirits, are very real. The results of being ignorant about the paranormal can be (I Peter 5:8–9) damning to you and others. People who deny the existence of the enemy are not prepared to fight adequately. There are varied responses to the paranormal (Luke 10: 17 – 20). Some people act like demons don't exist, so they are essentially leaving themselves defenseless. Some people accept the fact of demons existing, but they do not apply this knowledge to their lives. Wise people will not deny the reality of the paranormal and will be willing to investigate and be open-minded to this very important subject.

*Chapter 3*

# Reality of the Spirit World (We Believe You)

Paranormal experiences are fascinating to millions of people. There's a culture of people that enjoy different paranormal topics. More and more people are accepting that paranormal experiences are real.

Frequently, people will call, saying they know issues are going on in their house. Maybe there's darkness in the house, maybe there's demonic activity, or maybe they feel cursed or under attack in their personal life. Maybe there's an attachment of some kind of demon.

We know today that there is no question that there are all kinds of dark entities at work. We call them demons or ghosts. I think if most people were honest, they would believe in the paranormal. A recent survey showed that over 75% of the people in the world believe in things that they cannot see. They believe in the spirit world.

Many people believe when a person dies, they don't just die; they're not just put in the ground and stop living. Most people believe we have a soul, and our soul lives forever. I want you to know that the paranormal experiences that you're having can be a reality. People say to me all the time, "Well, I would love to reach out to you for help." Often people say, "I would like to talk to my pastor about this paranormal experience in my life, but I don't think they would believe me. He might think I am crazy." Some people have recurring dreams that are disturbing or evil. Maybe there is a poltergeist in your home and you are hearing strange noises, and there are things in your house moving around. Maybe your kids or your family are experiencing unusual activity. Many times, they'll say, "I'm really afraid to talk about it. I know if I tell these paranormal things, no one will believe me." Paranormal events are mysteries—things that you can't explain. Paranormal activity can be happening just to you, and maybe you're the only one in the home that is affected. Some people say, "I ask other people, like my husband and my kids, if they are experiencing this." and sometimes they'll say, "No, I'm not experiencing anything." Sometimes only one person can sense something. Other times, everyone in the family will be experiencing paranormal events.

There are a lot of unique things about this particular ministry. Being a pastor for over 42 years and pastoring mega churches, as well as being a police officer for 10 years, I not only believe you, but our team of professionals believes you too. I assure you; there's a lot of people out there that are experiencing paranormal activity. You may be afraid to tell your pastor, co-workers, or your wife or husband for fear they're going to think you are crazy. We hear that all the time.

We get many calls, hundreds of calls, from across the nation. This ministry is not just a wide ministry in America; it's also international. We get calls many times from Canada, Asia, Europe, Brazil, Mexico, etc.

The Bible tells us that paranormal activity is real, and the entire Bible is a book full of paranormal experiences. The Bible speaks about the supernatural and talks about the power of God, good angels, and dark angels. There's no better book for the paranormal than the word of God. Ephesians chapter 10 says, "Finally, my brethren, be strong in the Lord and the power of His might." and it says in the New

Testament Ephesians chapter 6 verse 11, "Put on the whole armor of God that you might be able to stand against the wiles of the devil." That little word wiles means tricks, schemes, or deceptions. Ephesians 6:12 is the key verse I want you to see. It says, "For we wrestle not against flesh and blood but against principalities." The word principality means dark things. It talks about the word principality, which denotes different levels of power and order in the dark kingdom. We have learned that demons have different functions and different levels of power. They have a hierarchy. In our conversations with demons, they have said to us that they can be promoted or demoted depending on their obedience and success. Ephesians 6:12 tells us, "For we wrestle not against flesh and blood, but against principalities, against powers, against the rulers of the darkness of this world, against spiritual wickedness in high places."

This verse emphasizes that the struggles and conflicts believers face are not merely against human opponents but against powerful, unseen spiritual entities. In Bible times, the phrase "high places" referred to places of worship of false gods. They were usually located on top of hills and mountains. Evil orgies and human sacrifices were common practices in these high places. Many believe that the author of this passage, the apostle Paul, could also be referring to wicked entities who have influenced important places such as religious organizations, educational systems, and government bureaucracies.

We believe you. The Bible makes it clear that paranormal activity is a reality. You may be in a battle between good and evil in your own personal life. Another reason we believe you is because of our own personal experiences. When you reach out to us in this ministry, I doubt that you're ever going to tell us anything that we haven't already heard. We've done hundreds of cases of different levels of paranormal activity. Some are more serious than others. Some are more dangerous than others. We have experienced many strange things. We get calls all the time about people having demonic issues, and we receive calls all the time about children being scratched and hurt in their home. We have traveled literally hundreds of thousands of miles to go investigate and see what's going on. And what makes us unique is that we're not just paranormal investigators but pastors. We will try to help you figure out not only what's going on, but we are willing to take it a step further. We come in, and we use the tools that God's given to us to help free you. We will help you to get freedom for you and your families from these demonic attacks in your life.

We've seen people levitate; we've gone into homes where we start praying over people where things move around in the house. We've helped people that continue to have the same dream, maybe a nightmare, repeatedly. Recently, we had a case where we helped a family, and everyone in the family, including the husband, the wife, and the three kids, were all having the exact same nightmare. That's not coincidental. That's not something that just happens; that's spiritual warfare. That is real paranormal activity. Be aware, because generally, if left undealt with, these types of things tend to escalate.

I've recently been helping people with spiritual warfare issues and many paranormal situations full time. I often get asked, "Is this stuff real?" Some people say, "No, I don't believe that there's any such thing as demons and creatures that live in the spirit world." And then you have some people that will say, "Everything bad that happens to me is caused by a demon." It is interesting you have two extremes.

You've heard it said, and it's also true in the paranormal field, that usually the truth is somewhere in the middle of those extremes.

After working over hundreds of paranormal cases, I can personally attest that demons are real. We can hear them, and we see objects move around many times. I was working in a case down in South Texas. We were in a very dark home. The demons were affecting one of the members of the family. The demon was telling him to hurt himself and telling him to go out and hurt someone else. We were sitting in the living room talking about what was going on in their lives. They began to tell us about the kinds of paranormal activity that was taking place in their home. My assistant was on the right of the man, and I was to his left. It was kind of a home where you could see the kitchen from the living room, and on the bar was a knife, kind of like a butcher knife. It was not very big, more of a medium-sized knife.

Because of my prior work in law enforcement, I pay attention to details when I go into a home. I generally look around to see if there are weapons and if the home is safe. I noticed this knife on the counter, and we started the interview and discussed demons. He began telling me how they were affecting him. They were sending him messages, and he was literally getting texts on his phone from this demon. He notified his cell phone company, and they could not find any trace of it. They could see where the texts were coming in, but they couldn't tell him what number the text was coming from. While we were having this discussion, I noticed the knife on the bar started moving a little. Not really fast, but an inch at a time, and it just kept moving and moving. I knew without a doubt the demon in that particular house was real, and I knew he was powerful. I also knew he wanted to kill us.

As I sat there for about 20 minutes, the knife had completely changed positions on the bar, and now the knife was pointed exactly at me. I knew in my heart, and I knew in my spirit, that the demon wanted to thrust that knife into me. I even had a vision of it where I saw the knife flying across the room and coming at me. And so, while we were talking, I literally said, "Just a minute, we need to do something." I said, "We need to pray." So, I prayed, and I looked toward that knife, and I said, “In the name of Jesus Christ, by the power of Jesus, that knife is not going to hurt anyone in this room.” I commanded the demon that was behind that knife, the ones that have been making that knife move, to get out of the room. I proclaimed, “We are protected by Jesus Christ; we are here under his authority, and Demon, you're going to lose this battle. You are not going to touch us.”

When we came to the house to visit these people, we had to open up the door, but demons were able to walk through the door. As we’ve mentioned before, they are intellectual beings and very smart and strategic. As genuine believers in Christ, we have been given authority and boldness to dismantle and resist demonic attacks that are aimed at us.

We know the Bible says in John chapter 10 verse 10 that “the Devil comes to steal, kill, and destroy. How does he do that? Usually, it's not going to be the Devil himself because he's big and he's busy. Most of the time, the actual devil doesn't get involved in our lives. He sends or assigns his demons. Remember that the devil is the commander-in- chief and the demons are like soldiers in his army. He assigns these demons into our lives and into our children's lives. Sometimes they're in spirit form where you can't see them, but sometimes they can manifest physically. They may look like a person or an animal.

Demons have all kinds of abilities to do this, and they're very strong. There are many different levels, but one of the things that we have discovered about demons is that their intent is to destroy us. Don't forget our God is more powerful than the devil. The Bible tells us that demons at one time were angels and explains how they rebelled against God. God kicked them out of heaven. In the spirit world, you have protection, good angels fighting against the bad angels. If your kids are dreaming about demons or they're actually seeing demons or orbs, take it seriously because these demons are real. They're intellectual beings; they're powerful, and they mean to do us harm.

We have also interviewed many witnesses who have also experienced or encountered demonic activities at physical locations. Demons can be attached to property as well as to a person. In our ministry, we are often asked to conduct blessings for houses or businesses. Recently, people from a dentist office in Corpus Christi, two businesses in my home town of Greenwood, Arkansas, and a church facility in Wichita, Kansas, asked for us to do a building cleansing for them. Property can be affected by negative energy from the past. Criminal activity such as rape, murder, and child molestation can create issues. Buildings or property that have been used for pagan worship or satanic rituals commonly need to be cleansed and blessed. Places where witchcraft has been performed are tainted. Places marked with pentagrams and even hidden symbols that conjure up evil can influence the property. Burial grounds and cultural rituals can also be problematic.

*Chapter 4*

# Dealing With Demons

Theologians and demonologists estimate that 8 to ten billion angels became demons. They operate as bullies and terrorists. Revelation 12:7-9 says, "And war broke out in heaven: Michael and his angels fought with the dragon; and the dragon and his angels fought, but they did not prevail, nor was a place found for them in heaven any longer. So, the great dragon was cast out, that serpent of old, called the Devil and Satan, who deceives the whole world; he was cast to the earth, and his angels were cast out with him."

## I. What demons possess:

Ephesians 6: 11-12 says, "Put on the whole armor of God, that you may be able to stand against the wiles of the devil. For we do not wrestle against flesh and blood, but against principalities, against powers, against the rulers of the darkness of this age, against spiritual hosts of wickedness in the heavenly places."

A. Position
B. Personality
C. Power
D. Purpose
E. Passion

## II. Why do demons attack a person or attach themselves to someone?

John 10:10 In my experience of exercising and casting out demons, they will try to argue with me that they have the right and authority to be connected to a particular person. They will often state that they have the right to be involved in the person's life. They frequently act as lawyers, presenting arguments.

A. Curses that have been placed on us through witchcraft
B. Generational sins (familiar spirits)
C. Opened portals from different kinds of sins
D. Assignments from Satan

## III. The most common and dangerous demons:

A. Demons of death
B. Demons of suicide
C. Demons of addiction
D. Demons of sexual perversion (homosexuality, transgender, adultery, pornography)
E. Demons of religion
F. Demons of infirmity
G. Demons of lies and confusion
H. Demons of rebellion
I. Demons of laziness
J. Demons of strife (cause disunity)
K. Demons of depression

## IV. What demons fear the most:

A. Satan
B. Jesus (according to John Hagee, Jesus cast out demons 76 times)

C. The Bible
D. Spirit-filled Christians
E. Prayer warriors
F. Demonologists and exorcism

## V. What it takes to conquer demons:

A. Spiritual authority
B. Spiritual knowledge
C. Spiritual truth
D. Spiritual boldness
E. Prayer and fasting

## VI. What can demons do?

A. Possess a lost person
B. Demonize or vex a Christian (22 scriptures use the word vex or vexed)
C. Oppress a Christian
D. Attach
E. Agitate
F. Speak to you
G. Confuse you
H. Convince you
I. Cause you to kill
J. Cause fear
K. Hurt you
L. Damage relationships
M. Live in animals or people
N. Go through walls
O. Take human form or animal form
P. Make you physically or mentally sick
Q. Make you angry and bitter
R. Make you sleepy

## VII. Three things demons cannot do to Christians:

A. Read your mind
B. Make you do anything you choose not to do
C. Kill you without God's permission

## VIII. How can demons be defeated?

A. Receive Christ
B. Realize the reality of them
C. Respect their power
D. Remember who we are in Christ
E. Resist the devil, James 4:7
F. Restrict Satan's opportunity to attack; give no place to the devil, Ephesians 4:27
G. Refuse to give in to temptation
H. Remove fear

## IX. A simple scriptural proclamation to speak against the devil and his demons:

"Hey demons, the blood of Jesus is against you, and so am I. You are not welcome here, and you must leave." There is power in the spoken word when given with boldness.

## XI. Conclusion:

Avoid the two extreme views about demons:

A. Ignore them
B. Glorify them

We must remember what I John 4:4 says: "You are of God, little children, and have overcome them, because He who is in you is greater than he who is in the world."

There are different definitions for demon, but the one that I think is most accurate is this. The definition of a demon is an intellectual being that was created by God, who rebelled against God and chose to join Satan. Theologians and demonologists estimate that there are 8 to 10 billion angels who became demons. We found this in the Bible. It says in Revelation 12:7–9, a war broke out in heaven, and Michael and his angels fought with the dragon, and the dragon and his angels fought, it says, but they did not prevail. There was no place for them in heaven any longer. So, the great dragon, referring to the devil or Satan, was cast out. The serpent of old is the devil. It is Satan who deceives the entire world. He was cast to the earth, and his angels were cast out with him. It is particularly important to understand here that at one time these demons were angels. They were serving God in heaven, but there was a great rebellion in heaven against God, and they chose to go against God.

People often ask me, "How do you describe a demon and how they work?" I would say they operate as bullies and terrorists. That is an effective way to describe them. We have all had to put up with bullies in school, and we live in a world where there's terrorists. That is a good description of who these demons are.

It is also important to understand that God created them as angels. They have intellectual abilities. We are going to discover several things about these creations from God, who at one time were all good but then chose to rebel in some way. Reading this, some would ask, "Why would God create something that would turn bad? One of the greatest gifts that God gives to all his creation was choice: a choice to serve him, a choice to do good, a choice not to do good, or not to serve him. And unfortunately, there was a huge army of angels who chose to follow Satan, the devil. He was originally created as an angel directly under God. When he rebelled, he convinced many angels to turn their backs on God and join him. Literally, we are fighting an army today of darkness in a battle that you may not be able to see. Sometimes you can see them, sometimes you can't, but you just think about it. If this is true and there's as many as ten billion demons in the world, we better pay attention to that.

Demons are intellectual beings that were created by God. The Bible gives us a little more description about these demons in Ephesians 6:11–12. It says to put on the whole armor of God that you may be able to stand against the wiles of the devil. That word wiles in the

Greek means trickery of the devil. It says to "put on the armor of God, that you might be able to stand against the trickery or the wiles of the devil." It continues, "For we do not wrestle against flesh and blood, but against principalities, against powers, against the rulers of darkness." In this age, the word "principalities" is a word that describes order or rank. We see that there are various kinds of demons. They have different passions and different courses, different personalities, and different purposes to come against people. This is what it means when the Bible talks about wrestling against principalities and against powers, against rulers of darkness. Notice Satan and demons are referred to as rulers of the darkness. Anything that you see that is referred to as good or light is referring to God.

They have a position in order. I would say it's kind of like an army.

These demons have rank and file, and it's pretty interesting as we deal with them. We have dealt with them in over 400 cases of exorcisms and doing deliverance. In our ministry, we have dealt with demons of all diverse kinds of levels, different kinds of power, and they have various levels of authority. For instance, when I moved back to Greenwood to operate our ministry out of Arkansas,

I was asked to help with a case there. It was at a business in downtown Greenwood, in an old building. The people in the building said that they were struggling with seeing things in the building. They were also hearing things in the building. In fact, some of their children had tried to spend the night there. They were horrified by some of the things that the demons had said to them and literally had run them out of the building. When they asked me if I would go into the building to do a cleansing, of course we agreed to do that. Late on a Friday night, my team went into that building. As we were upstairs in the attic area, I heard very clearly a demon that responded to me.

And he said to me that he was indeed the demon that oversaw the area and that he was not going to give up any ground to us. In fact, he made the statement, "You used to live here. You've been gone a long time. Things have changed in this town." As you're going to see in different places in this book, this is only one of the many conversations I've had with demons. When we do this ministry of exorcisms and deliverance, we've had to learn to be prepared for conflict. These things come against us, and it's a battle every time.

How much of a battle is it? Well, it depends on which demons we're battling. There are some demons that are much easier to battle than other demons. When you think about this, think about position. They have position, but they also have different personalities, different purposes, and different places. You're going to see that demons have different personalities. Some demons are more direct. Some of them will hide, and some of them will try to deny certain things. Some will directly attack you with words or physical attacks. Some will avoid confrontation. Some will just come at you to embarrass you or make fun of you.

When we talk about what the demons possess, we know they have position, they have organization, they have rank, and we know they have personality. I have discovered that no two demons are ever the same, you know, and that's just like with God's creation. Just as no two human beings are ever the same, I've discovered that no two demons are ever the same. They might have some of the same assignments, but they're different. And I want to say, not only do they have position and personality, but they also have power. There are various levels. I mentioned this a while ago. We've dealt with demons that have a little power, and we've dealt with demons that have a lot of power. When I'm working with Janie, my ministry assistant, and we are in the middle of doing a deliverance and exorcism, we will always try to seek out the most powerful demon, or what we call the alpha demon or the head demon. There's usually more than one demon in a person or even in a building. They run in packs. Our ministry teams have a ranking system between 1 and 10. And many times in the middle of dealing with this demon, either myself or another team member will say, "This is probably a 5 or 7 or 8." What we mean by that is how much power they seem to have. When you understand demons, you understand that they have rank, they have order, they have personality, they can be funny, they can be mean, they can be serious, they can be naughty, they can be dirty. It is obvious that you're not just dealing with different personalities but also different powers. The word "principalities" is strong when it talks about rank

and different kinds of demons. But it also says, as we're reading there in Ephesians 6 about principalities, it also says "against powers." Demons have shown their power. I've learned the demons like to show their power. Sometimes when we're doing deliverance, these demons will try to show their power.

When I was pastoring out in Big Spring, Texas, many, many years ago,

I had a lady that was demon-possessed who came to my office, and the demons started speaking through her. She said to me, “If you would like, I could make all those books come off your shelf right now. “As soon as she said that, the books on my shelf started sliding from one side to the other. And there was commotion there. I immediately told her, “Stop, stop. I don't want to see your power. I'm not interested in what you can do.” The movement stopped. I would say in several cases, as we've worked across the country, one in Kansas comes to mind, one in Texas, North Carolina, and Kentucky, we have had the power to limit what they can do.

Sometimes when we're doing a deliverance, the demons will try to show off their power to cause us to be afraid or to cause us to get sidetracked. Many times, we've seen levitation. We had a case in Kansas where a person that we were praying over was literally lifted up. We were in a conference room, and literally the person was lifted up over the conference table. I, at once, took charge and told that demon that he could not continue to do that. Even the chair itself was experiencing levitation. We pulled the chair back to the ground, and we told the demon that you can no longer do this. I was in another part of Kansas, and I was delivering a young woman. As I was praying over her, she was sitting on the couch, and I had my hands on her shoulders as I was praying over her. Suddenly, she lifted up. Her entire body was being lifted off the couch. I could give you many other examples of levitation. They're showing off. The demons are showing you that they have power.

Demons frequently try to demonstrate their power. We've been in places where things, like glass, have been broken. We were doing a full exorcism down in Corpus Christi, Texas, on a young girl, and her mom and dad, and family were there. When we were praying for the demons to leave, they were literally arguing with us. Suddenly, the entire house began to shake. The electricity was affected, and the lights began to flash. There were all kinds of strange noises. I'll be honest with you: at that moment in time, you might have thought you were in a Hollywood movie. Oftentimes people ask me, “Are the things you see in movies true?” Well, sometimes they're not.

Sometimes they're just trying to make it sensational. I have to be honest with you: many times, and many things you see in the horror movies are somewhat accurate. Demons do actually have the power to do many things that are strange and terrifying.

I’ve said that demons are intellectual. They're smart, they have power, and they have personality. They have position, but they also have a purpose. It's important to know that demons are not just floating around looking for something to do. They have a master.

Their master is Satan. In reality, they have two masters. When we deal with demons, they'll tell us that their master is Satan. But if you really pin them down, they will tell you, I have two masters. They know that. God is also the master, and they don't like to admit that, but we love to remind them that they really have two masters, but their immediate supervisor is Satan. We find that demons have been given assignments. They're not just floating around out there with no purpose.

If you're battling a demon in your life today, there's a reason for that. It's not just accidental. We're going to have some good information about portals. Portals are openings or opportunities. But make no mistake about it; demons have assignments, and they have been assigned by their masters. Remember the rank and file and that there's a reason. We try to understand what kind of power the demons possess, but figure out what their purpose is. Many demons possess passion. Let me tell you, they are very passionate; they are not playing around. I know a lot of people who will say, “Well, I'm not afraid of these demons, and I'll go take these demons on.” Let me just tell you, be careful there. These demons are passionate about what they do. Some people ask, "Why don't exorcisms work all the time?" This is a spiritual battle. It requires much prayer and work. Demons are very passionate about what they do. The good news is our team and ministry are very passionate, too. We get on airplanes and fly across the country to go help people. We're not going to play games either. If you're going to be effective in fighting these demons, you have to match their passion.

Many times, when I get back from working on a case, my son will ask, "Why did the demons target or attach themselves to the client or property?" In my experience of being an exorcist and doing deliverance ministry and casting out demons, they will oftentimes argue with me that they have the right and authority to be in a particular person. I've said that many times. Demons are like lawyers in some ways. They like to argue and debate. They will often insist that they have the right to be involved in a person's life. They often will argue their point and make an argument for them being there.

We know when we start investigating that we must figure it out. We ask ourselves why that being is there. Why are they arguing that they have the right and authority? Well, there can be several reasons. Here are a few. There are some people that have had curses that have been placed on them through witchcraft. This is the situation with many cases we've handled. The person may have made someone angry, or for some reason they became a target of a curse from someone in their family or an acquaintance that cursed them through witchcraft.

Another reason that we uncover many times for a demon being in a person's life is generational sins. The Bible refers to them as familiar spirits. Some spirits may have been in a family for many, many years. We were in a place up in Kansas, a small town close to Wichita, and we were trying to get a demon out of a person. We were in a battle.

We were exorcising the demon, and the demon had told me he'd been in the family a long time. I asked him how many years he had been in the bloodline of this family. And he replied, 1600 years. Well, I think that's very possible. The reason I believe that it is possible is because these demons go back to the beginning of time. They may have been with a particular family for centuries. They go way back, and they can be attached to people or places through many generations. In one case, we discovered that a deal was made with Satan generations ago. In this case, it was several hundred years, and the demon said to us, “I can prove to you that I've been in this family,” and he started naming the names of several people that he had killed or caused to die. There was a member of this family there while we were doing the exorcism that later admitted to me, “I kind of doubted your ability. I kind of doubted if this thing was legit or not. But when it started naming the names of people that were in our family many, many years ago and that they had died suspicious deaths, I knew then that this stuff was real. This demon knew exactly what he was talking about.”

It could be a curse, it could be a generational connection, but it also could be open portals. And we're going to have an entire chapter on that. Why are you under attack? It is an assignment from Satan.

Always remember that the demons are accountable to Satan himself. When you think about these demons that we talked about—who they are, the power they have—we've talked about some of the reasons why they're working in someone’s life.

I want to mention to you that there are many different kinds of demons. We could spend a lot of time on this. I could write an entire book just on the different kinds of demons there are but let me just give you some examples. Some of the most common and dangerous demons that we have discovered are demons of death.

They're all about death. By the way, demons love death, and demons can cause someone to commit suicide. A demon of death can also work through sickness or it can cause accidents, but his whole purpose is to cause death. We've gone into some locations that have a history of deaths and have no connection to the families that live there, but just about everybody who lives there has to deal with death in that particular place.

There are many demons of suicide, and I think that's one of the most common. We also seem to battle with demons of addiction. Now, I'm not saying that every addiction is caused by a demon, but make no mistake about it, there are demons of addiction. There are demons of sexual perversion, homosexuality, and demons promoting the transgender movement. They convince people that God made a mistake in their identity. I believe that these demons, demons of sexual perversion, try to create perversion through sex. And one thing that I would say here is that demons are very sexual.

The one that we discovered that surprised us a lot was what we call a demon of religion. And we discovered that there are demons that have fake religion; they will convince the person that they're from God. Many times, when we go to a case, we start to exorcise the demons. The demon will start telling the people, "These are the bad people." They do not want the people to trust the ministry team. You know, we're good people! We're of God, trying to help set people free. They're of Satan; they're of the devil. But remember, demons have no problem lying. They are also sometimes able to convince a person that they're really Christians when they're not. Satan tries to blind people to their true needs. There are all kinds of other demons.

There's a demon of rebellion the Bible talks about in the Old Testament in the book of 1 Samuel. It says that rebellion is the sin of witchcraft. They're demons of rebellion, and these are demons that cause people to rebel. This is especially true in adolescence and children. We've seen that there are demons of infirmity that make people sick.

Other times we've experienced demons of strife. Demons love to tear down relationships. Demons are jealous; they're also very territorial.

They don't want you to have a good marriage. The demons don't want you to get along with your kids. They're masters at disturbing relationships, and we see that in many cases.

There are demons of depression. These demons are enormously powerful. They can cause depression and oppression. They oppress people to the point where sometimes they don't even want to live anymore. They don't want to do anything or go anywhere. The demons want them to just wallow in their misery and sadness.

Demons want to make people feel hopeless and like there is no way to improve their situation. We have been in homes that looked like hoarders lived there. People look around and don't know where to start. They become overwhelmed and just don't do anything. My assistant Janie pointed out that in some cases we've been dealing with what we call demons of laziness. They make someone lazy to the point where they don't want to do anything in life.

We talk about demons and how they were created by God. They have passion, they have personality, and they have purpose. They have assignments, and there's distinct kinds of them. Satan will assign diverse kinds of demons to your particular case. You have to be very careful. With that being said, what can demons do? Demons can possess a lost person. When we say a lost person, we're talking about a person that has no relationship with Christ. They're wide open. We believe that a person who is not a Christian, a person who has no relationship with God, no connection with God, can certainly experience full possession. Full possession means that a demon, or demons, have complete control over our mind and our bodies. This can be extremely dangerous because a person who is completely possessed by demons may have no control over what they do or say. These demons can command them to go and hurt someone and to kill people. That's why our team has to be very careful when we go to do exorcisms because sometimes, we're battling demons that have literally possessed a person.

Demons can also demonize or vex a person. Even a Christian can be influenced by a demon. My theology says a person who's a Christian cannot be completely controlled by Satan. But don't misunderstand this; demons can vex a Christian. The word vex is found twenty-two times in the Scriptures, and it means to have influence in their lives in different ways. So even a Christian can be demonized or vexed. A lot of people in the church say, "Well, if I'm a Christian and I'm a member of the church and all that, then the demons can't bother me." Let me tell you something. That's a straight-out lie. Being a pastor for four decades, I can tell you that's one of the lies of the devil—to tell you that you don't have to worry about demons if you're a Christian.

That's not true. They can oppress a Christian. They can be attached to a Christian. We call them attachments, and sometimes we must work to get rid of them.

These demons can talk to people. They can speak to you. They can confuse you. They confuse people. They can cause someone to kill and do horrible things. These demons can live in humans. I have found that demons prefer to find something living to inhabit. Now it is true that sometimes demons will be connected to a property like a forest or certain lands because of things that happened on that land. They can be in certain places, but in our experience, they like to live in people and sometimes in animals. I get asked all the time, "Can demons live inside animals?" Sure, they can. People say,

"Well, do you respect these demons?" Well, I know they have power and can do things that humans cannot do. Many times, we see these demons. They come through walls. They go through windows; they go through doors. Remember they were angels at one time, and they have a lot of power. These demons can take human form. How powerful are they? They can turn into what looks like a human you recognize and trick you sometimes. They'll do that sometimes to trick you into thinking it was someone you loved and someone you cared about.

They can make you physically or mentally sick. They can bring diseases to you.

I remember when I was doing an exorcism in Wichita, Kansas, of a young girl who was a hairdresser. It was on a Friday, and we were all about to go home when we heard someone banging on the doors of the church. It was a young lady and two of her friends that wanted us to help her. They said that she was possessed by Satan. We really weren't prepared to do an exorcism, but we felt like we needed to help her. So, for the next two hours, we battled the demon in this young girl's life. In the middle of doing the deliverance ministry, she literally reached up and struck me in the chest. Sometimes these can get very physical. Even though there were two of her friends that were trying to hold her back, she'd gotten physical, and she made a move, and she struck me in the chest. She started laughing a hideous laugh, a demonic laugh. She asked, "How does it feel to get hit in your sore heart?" A couple of years before that, I had found out that I have a heart condition. It's not really that sore, but I do take medicine.

Obviously that demon knew that was a source for a sore spot in my body, and they made fun of that. When that demon asked, "How does it feel to get hit in your sore heart?" my response back to them was this, "How does it feel to know that you can't stop my heart from beating? Only God can do that."

We ended up having to go to their home later to complete the exorcism. But by God's grace, she was delivered from these demons, and there were several. They can not only affect you physically, but they can affect you emotionally. They affect many people mentally. I want to encourage you to read the chapter in this book that talks about mental illness and the difference between paranormal and demonic activity and mental illness. There is a difference, but a person can have one or the other or both.

Dealing with demons is something that can be extremely dangerous and complicated. Whether you realize it or not, they're around, and they're working.

*Chapter 5*

# How to Make Demons Afraid of You

**Isaiah 41:10 (NKJV)**

**"Fear not**, for I *am* with you; Be **not** dismayed, for I *am* your God. I will strengthen you, yes, I will help you, I will uphold you with My righteous right hand.'"

What are you most afraid of in your life? God does not want us to live in fear. In fact, it's been said that there are 365 scriptures in the Bible that tell us not to fear, one for each day of the year. Yet we all have fears. There are a myriad of phobias. Many people are afraid of flying on airplanes. Some people are afraid of heights or speaking in front of crowds. People can be afraid of dogs, snakes, storms, small spaces, and the dark. One of the most common fears is the fear of dying.

Many people also have a fear of Satan and his demons. There are a few things of which I am afraid, but demons are not one of them.

Since I have spent so much of my life on airplanes, I have had to encourage many people sitting near me to not be afraid. One time, as I was boarding an early morning flight, I noticed a well-dressed, professional-looking man who was already seated. As I walked by him, our eyes made contact, and a demon inside him responded by growling. I immediately replied back to him by saying out loud, "Shut up, you dirty demon," as I continued to walk by him. As I prepared to be seated, a young lady approached me and asked, "Did I see that man growl at you? Did you say to him, 'Shut up, you dirty demon'"?

I replied, "Yes, ma'am." She asked if it was safe for her to be on this flight. She said she could definitely make other plans. I told her she could stay by me and she would have nothing to worry about. She asked the passenger next to me if she could change seats with him. Later in the flight, I went to the restroom, and as I exited the bathroom, I was surprised to see her standing right next to the bathroom door. I asked her if she was okay, and she said, "Yes, but you told me to stay next to you, and that is what I am going to do until the plane lands." When we landed, she was relieved and thanked me for watching over her and keeping her safe.

When God called me into this deliverance ministry, I knew it would include dealing with darkness, performing exorcisms, and having to deal with demons in many situations. Being afraid was no option for me if I was going to be successful in this work.

The devil and his demons operate effectively off of negative energy produced by fear. Many people are introduced to fear through horror movies or by personal experiences in their lives. Horror movies are extremely popular and are meant to create fear. People are drawn to them.

Being afraid of some things can be dangerous. You may be afraid to have surgery, but it may be necessary to save your life. The same can be true about spiritual surgery, which is what deliverance or exorcism really is. Our goal is to remove darkness or evil entities out of persons or properties. As we have worked over 400 cases, we have experienced God's power and protection first hand in many different situations.

Demons are really limited when we choose not to be afraid of them.

Growing up, my dad taught me not to be afraid of anyone. He said that people can see fear in your eyes. I was also taught this principle while being trained in law enforcement. Some people and demons can read your fear and will react to you accordingly. Anyone who is called to do deliverance ministry must learn how to conquer their fear.

In one of our cases, we were brought to a place in Arkansas to help a man that had been in prison twice for murder and selling drugs.

When I first encountered him, it would have been easy to be intimidated by his demeanor and evil tattoos all over his body. I can assure you, that while I was sizing him up, he was also sizing me up. He was not going to allow anyone to help him that he did not respect. He would not have respected me if I was afraid of him. With a lot of work, our team was able to help him and his family overcome a very dark and dangerous situation.

Remember this, Zachariah 4:6b says, "This is the word of the LORD to Zerubbabel: 'Not by might nor by power, but by my Spirit,' Says the LORD of hosts." There is a huge difference in being confident in God's power to overcome the power of the devil and his demons versus trusting in your own might or power. Arrogance and pride will result in your defeat.

## Five Ways How to Make Demons Afraid of You

1. Remember who made you. You have been created in God's image. You are special to God. You have been created by God with a purpose.
2. Realize what demons can and cannot do. The statement that knowledge is power is certainly true in dealing with demonic situations. For example, a demon cannot read your mind. A demon cannot force himself into your life. He must have your permission or a right to be there. They must be invited in or come in through a portal that is opened in your life.

3. Refuse to give in to fear. Don't be impressed or intimidated by their actions. Don't be influenced by their threats or pleas. Often, when we are helping people to get rid of their demons, the demons will try to scare us by making things move or causing people to levitate. Don't be afraid or get distracted. Often when we are casting demons out of people, they will try to show off by causing electricity to go off and on, or they might cause a picture to fall off the wall or windows or doors to slam shut. Once, in Corpus Christi, Texas, we were casting out demons from a young girl, and the house began to shake and the lights went off and on. If you had been there with us, you might have thought you were in the middle of a horror movie.

Their goal was to sidetrack us and cause us to be afraid and leave. However, we refused to give in to fear.

4. Respond to the demons with belief and boldness that you do not have to let them have their way. In our deliverance process, we teach people that there is power in the spoken word. The demons hate it when they are spoken to with authority.

5. Remind the demons that there are twice as many good angels as bad angels. When we call on God for help, He will dispatch good angels to help us. You are not alone in your fight against these demons.

I can assure you that you will not see the truth taught in this chapter in other places or from other paranormal teams.

## Practical Things to Help You Not be Afraid

- Leave on a lamp. Demons thrive in darkness.

- Play praise music. Demons do not like music that praises God.
- Put your Bible near you. Read scripture out loud and pray. Demons hate to hear scripture.
- Speak out loud to the demons and tell them they are not welcome. Say, "I command you to leave in the name of Jesus!" Remember, there is power in the spoken word when given with authority and boldness.
- Remember 1 John 4:4 says, "Ye are of God, little children, and have overcome them, because greater is he that is in you, than he that is in the world."

*Chapter 6*

# How Demons Gain Access (Portals)

When we talk about a portal, we are talking about an opening in our life. We are talking about anything that the devil and demons can use to justify their attachment or possession of a person. In this chapter, we will be talking about portals and pathways. Portals will cause us trouble and allow these dirty demonic entities in our lives. We are going to discuss how some portals can enter your life and cause havoc. Portals are not in someone's life accidentally. Many times, we do things in our lives to invite them in.

When we talk to a client, we try to determine the opening that Satan used to claim a right to be there. If someone is in a bad paranormal situation, they may also be in a church where their pastor may not know enough to help them. The pastor may be afraid and doesn't want to help with their paranormal issues because of fear the demons may come after him or his family. We are not afraid to help them, so we listen and take time to discover where the demonic influence began to take root.

The devil gives the demons assignments into your life, and there can be many reasons you may have a demon in your life. Instead of full possession, you could have oppression. Demons love to oppress and vex. Many Christians say when I got saved, that closed all the portals in my life to Satan. I know many Christians who are not possessed but are oppressed or demonized. If you are a Christian, God has your soul, and your soul is sealed until the day of redemption, but

Satan can infect your mind, your emotions, and your health.

Ephesians 4:30 says, “And do not grieve the Holy Spirit of God, by whom you were sealed for the day of redemption.” We are talking about those who are truly saved, not someone who says I am a Christian because I believe in God. The devil and his demons believe in God. We have talked to hundreds of demons, and they fear and believe in God. But unless you’ve given your heart to Jesus Christ, your soul is at risk. When we go fight these demons, we do not carry sage and ten pounds of salt; we take the name of Jesus. We don't have to bring salt, because we are the salt of the earth and the light of the world! Matthew 5 says, “Ye are the salt of the earth: but if the salt has lost his savour, wherewith shall it be salted? It is thenceforth good for nothing, but to be cast out, and to be trodden under foot of men. Ye are the light of the world. A city that is set on a hill cannot be hid.”

There is an authority that God has given to every believer and not just to us. True believers have an advantage in fighting demons because they have been given spiritual authority. Demons know that if they are exorcised and made to leave, they will be held accountable to the devil, and their mission is a failure. The Bible tells us in John 10:10 that Satan had come to kill and destroy. There are a lot of other things out there that can open the door. Remember, a portal is an opening into your life for the devil to come in.

Portals can be caused by something fun that we like to do. Drugs, alcohol, sex, pornography, and playing with a Ouija Board are examples of things that can start out as fun but can tragically open the door to something dangerous and dark. Often it is hard to close a portal and keep it closed once it has been opened. Demons will always be around us and are more than ready to enter our lives.

Through working on many cases, we have discovered many ways

that demons have come into people's lives.

Over the years, I have been told by demons many different reasons and excuses that they claim give them the right to enter and remain in the person's life. They have argued the fact that they have been given permission to work in the lives of these people. Portals can expand and reach other problem areas. Once a demon has started working in your life, it will study you and discover other areas of weakness to attack.

The Ouija board is one thing teenagers and adults both find fascinating. Many parents and grandparents buy these for their families, thinking they are innocent and harmless. Store owners tell us it is a great seller during the Christmas holidays. There is a particular demon that is assigned to Ouija boards; his name is Zozo. But often, other malevolent spirits will also come when people call. Demons are very powerful, and when someone gets on the Ouija board or spirit board, then they are knocking on the door of the spirit world. I know there are a lot of people who say, "I am missing my mom or my dad" or, "My best friend was killed in a car wreck, and I thought if I got the Ouija board, I could talk to them again." What I will tell you is that you will not be talking to your mom, dad, or friend. It will be a demon pretending to be them. The spirit board literally knocks on the door of the spirit world and says, "Hey, I am interested in you." The devil and the demons will jump on this opportunity to come into your life.

We have worked in several cases where demons have come into women's lives through abortion. Demons are all about death. In one very difficult exorcism, we dealt with a young woman who had several abortions. She had become demon-possessed. As we were battling these demons, we were told that a demon had entered her life each time she had an abortion. They felt like they had the right to be in her life because she had endorsed death. They identified themselves as demons of death. It took several sessions with her to get rid of her death demons. We should all realize that our actions can definitely be a doorway to the demonic.

Another dangerous portal is embracing a false religion or cult or being part of a movement that is not scriptural. We often deal with religious demons. These are demons that use and operate in the realm of religious people. Recently, a client brought a Bible to show me that had been placed in a family member's home. They did not know where it came from, but they felt like something was not right with it. Our team came to the conclusion that a spell had been placed on the Bible. Satan has no problem working with religious items, and demons are often found in church buildings. We are called on a regular basis to cleanse and remove darkness from church facilities.

Religious demons can cause confusion and twist the scriptures to manipulate people or cause strife. We have met several people who have been convinced by demons that they are Jesus. Another time, a person claimed to be the apostle Paul and wanted to take over the church. Keep in mind that demons do not fear the church, but they do really fear Jesus!

I want to mention one of the common portals is rebellion. The Bible declares in I Samuel 15:23 that rebellion is "like unto the sin of witchcraft." Allowing a rebellious spirit to have dominion in your life can be inviting demonic activity to come into your life. If you are a parent or grandparent, you definitely need to take action to remove the rebellious attitude. In my personal opinion, not disciplining children can open them up for demonic influence. We are living in a culture of rebellion today and turning away from the word.

There is another portal called a familiar spirit. Familiar spirits are real, and I know many families that will have some type of familiar spirit. Familiar spirits are spirits that have been passed down from generation to generation and are sometimes easy to spot. For example, if your dad was an alcoholic and you are an alcoholic and now your son has become an alcoholic, these are patterns.

Sometimes anger or pornography issues are passed down through generations. When I was growing up in Arkansas, they would say, "Well, that family has bad blood in them," and what they meant by that was that for generations they seem to have the same problems with alcohol and drugs. We worked in Kansas, where this demon told us he had been in the family for 1,600 years. The demon started naming all the people in the bloodline that he had caused to commit suicide. He took credit for all those suicides, and the family confirmed that many of their loved ones had in fact committed suicide. We live in a culture that doesn't take the devil seriously.

We must be careful about sexual encounters. We assisted a lady in Texas who had a sexual relationship with a man who was demon-possessed. In the middle of the encounter, she reported she could feel the demon leave the man and enter her body. Her life became a mess, and she reached out to our ministry to ask for help. I don't care how they look or talk or how much money they have in their life, people can be a tool of the devil in your life. Many times, evil people can open portals to your life, so beware of who you are dealing with.

Unfortunately, sexual molestation and sexual perversion are other common portals that we see. When people are molested or raped, they sometimes feel embarrassed or ashamed and will not seek help. They may feel used and angry and can become bitter as well as harbor unforgiveness. Their self-esteem can be damaged, and they may become withdrawn or depressed. Demons prey on the weak. We have helped many people deal with this across several states, including Georgia, North Carolina, Kentucky, Kansas, Maryland, and Texas. We were also able to help a lady in Kansas that was involved in beastiality, and she attracted several demon attachments. These abnormal sexual issues oftentimes open portals.

Another common portal is unforgiveness. This is a very common problem when trying to remove the demons from a person's life. Forgiveness allows people to heal and closes this portal.

Hatred is another portal. Many times, people have a legitimate reason to hate. But as a result of hate, a doorway for demons is opened. After all, demons are full of hate.

We have discovered that idle hands or laziness can be used by demons as well.

The Living Bible Translation says in Proverbs 16:27, "Idle hands are the devil's workshop; idle lips are his mouthpiece."

Another way that demons can gain access and influence is through witchcraft, voodoo, black magic, and occult practices. Spells and curses can be placed on a person by someone. We have been working with a client in New Jersey who became enemies with a person who had been his friend. She was a witch, and she told him that she was going to destroy his life by putting spells on him with her black magic. At first, he thought it was a joke and wasn't worried about it. Then his life took a turn for the worst. He lost his job; he lost his health and all his friends. Until then, he thought he had a perfect life. We are in the process of determining which spells and curses need to be broken so we can counter them with prayer and blessings. These kinds of portals need to be taken seriously because there is an explosion of witchcraft and black magic in our world today.

Demons can use electronics to open portals in our lives. We were asked to assist in a case in Minnesota that involved a pastor and his wife. They were serving in a very large church. They were doing a gaming ministry. They would connect with people across the country on the sites. They would share the gospel with them. The pastor's wife got connected with a demon-possessed man that lived in Texas. He was able to draw her away from her family and church to have a relationship with him. Our research showed that he was into some very dark and evil practices, including Satanism. We need to be careful of gaming sites, dating sites, and chat rooms or blogs that enable you to connect with people you don't know.

I want to empower you with some information on how to close a portal that has been opened in your life that has allowed demonic activity.

- First, you must **realize** that there is an issue. Otherwise, you will not get any help.
- Second, you should do **research** to find out where and how the portal was opened.
- Third, you must be willing to **remove** the portal from your life.
- Fourth, you must refuse to **reopen** the portal again.

*Chapter 7*

# Signs of Paranormal Activity in Your Life

As we've stated, paranormal activity is something that is outside of what is natural. Paranormal activity is not something you can necessarily take a picture of, although often it has been caught on camera. There are diverse kinds of paranormal activity. Paranormal activity cannot necessarily be seen, but make no mistake about it; it can be experienced. Paranormal activity can be felt. Evidence such as bruises and scratches can be seen. You can occasionally feel, see, hear, or smell paranormal activity. Moving objects can be caught on camera. There are many signs that could indicate the presence of unseen entities.

Many people are afraid to tell other people about what they are experiencing because they are worried other people will think they are crazy. I think it is important that whoever is reading this understands that they are not alone. Paranormal activity can and does happen to all kinds of people. We need to understand that paranormal activity can take place anywhere. Frequently, paranormal things come from a spiritual world that is not seen by many people.

Some people would say, "Well, I am just going to excuse myself from the spiritual world. I'm just going to be in the physical world." Some folks may say, "I am not open to the paranormal, and I don't have any belief in its existence, and I'm just going to ignore it so it doesn't affect me." Even if you don't realize it, the spiritual world is around you! The scripture says very clearly that we are in a fight, a spiritual battle. There is a spiritual war going on, whether we admit it or not. And more than that, there is a spiritual world, and we live in that world.

What are some signs of paranormal activity? I am going to give many examples of different signs of paranormal activity. I'm going to start with some of the most common ones that people ask me about all the time. Many have experienced disappearing objects. I kind of laugh about this a little, but it is true. I've had things in my own life disappear, like keys, and we never found them. All of us misplace our keys from time to time, but sometimes things completely disappear or get moved to a very unusual place. I personally believe that both angels and demons have the ability to do this. Entities may do this to irritate or harass you or to show you that they are there. They may be hindering you from going to do something important. Angels may hide things as well, in order to keep you from danger. Angels may be trying to cause you to end up at a certain place and time for a divine appointment.

Another sign of paranormal activity is a sense of something in the room and smelling odors. As we have done cases all over America, as well as internationally, people have reported that when something's going on in the spiritual realm, they sense certain odors or smell something unusual. It's interesting regarding the subject of ghosts and how sometimes people will smell the same perfume that their grandmother, or their mom, or their daughter wore in the past. Many times, people will talk about smelling cigars or cigarette smoke. One of the more common things that we hear is that they smell sulfur. It is kind of interesting when we think about darkness; we think about Satan, hell, and the smell of sulfur. Not just once or twice, but many times people report the smell of sulfur.

Sometimes people say that when they are experiencing paranormal activity, electrical interference occurs. It is not uncommon for spiritual beings, including demons, to make the lights go off. One time

I was going to preach a revival in Louisiana and I checked into a fairly nice motel, not a cheap place. As soon as I walked into the motel room, I flipped on the light switch. As soon as I turned it on, something flipped it off. I went back over, and I flipped it on again.

Well, as soon as I walked away, I literally saw the switch move back off again. I knew then that I was seeing paranormal activity. I was not just imagining that the light switch went off. There have been many other cases that we worked on where we knew electrical interference was being caused by paranormal activity. Many times, we would be talking before doing deliverance ministry or we were in the middle of doing a house blessing or cleansing, and the lights would begin to flash.

We sometimes see paranormal activity portrayed in movies. I often get asked if those movies are true. While there are some things that are made up and exaggerated, much of the stuff you see in those movies could possibly happen.

Another sign of paranormal activity is being attacked physically in your body. Many people report being pushed. Many people tell us they're being touched sexually. They tell us they are being physically assaulted or raped by something unseen. They have bruises on their bodies. I've had many cases where people have been injured by paranormal activity. For instance, many times people have said, “I felt something push me down the stairs” or “I was tripped by something on the steps.” Another thing we commonly hear about would be physical attacks like scratches. I have never personally been scratched, but my associate Janie has been scratched.

Many people on our team have been physically attacked while

working on a case. Once in a very intense exorcism, in our third session of exorcising this lady, we circled her. Our entire team formed a circle, and we were praying and using the anointing oil. I was using a particular process that I use in doing exorcisms, and suddenly one of our team members got kicked hard from the back. She was thrust forward nearly on top of the person we were praying for. She said, “Something just kicked me in the back.” We lifted her shirt, and on her back was a huge footprint. I would guess around a size 12 man- sized footprint.

We must be careful when our team goes in to minister to people so that we don't get hurt. When we are in the middle of paranormal cases, we take precautions up a notch. I've had a couple cases where some people have indicated that something grabs hold of the steering wheel and tries to steer it head-on into another car. I've had other people say that the accelerator sticks in the car that they've been in and that a demon or some entity was trying to make the car accelerate and cause a crash.

I want to talk a little bit about other signs of paranormal activity in a person's life. We get many reports of ghosts, demons, djin, apparitions, sightings of the slender man, and shadow people. You're not crazy if you see things like this. You need to take it seriously.

Sometimes children are sensitive in this area. Every time this happens to a child; your radar should go off. I don't know about other paranormal ministries or teams, but we have been told that an entity has come in the form of a little girl or child. There is something that makes you want to just reach out to them. We must be careful, because sometimes demons appear in the form of a little girl to seem harmless. You also need to pay close attention to what your children are telling you. If your children are saying, “There's a monster in my closet” or “There’s a big, slender man that comes to the foot of my bed," listen to them. Many people claim kids have imaginary friends, and sometimes they do. Ask for details, and if that child can give you details on how tall they are, what they're wearing, if they have a hat on, or what their face looks like. If they are carrying on conversations with something unseen, ask them what they were talking about.

Janie and I worked on a case down in Texas with a family member. That family member reported that he knew something was watching him because he could see red eyes at night in the dark. Wherever he went, those red eyes followed him. As we all know, that is not normal, and that should absolutely be a warning that there's paranormal activity going on in this person's life.

Many times, children draw pictures. If your child is drawing dark images, that should be a sign. We have worked on more than 50 cases where kids all of a sudden feel compelled to draw things they are seeing or dreaming that are scaring them. Some people feel drawn to movies and books, and media that are dark. Some people will draw symbols of death and evil all around them.

Another sign of paranormal activity is phantom sounds of people walking or moving or chains rattling. Basements and cellars are known for having disembodied voices. Sometimes people will report hearing people having conversations, but there is no one there. They can understand what they're talking about, and they can hear people talking to each other. Many times, in the middle of the night, people will hear someone say their name, and they will get up to see who is there, and no one is there. These sounds may be signs of paranormal activity.

Other signs of paranormal activity are orbs and cold spots. Many times, paranormal activity is seen in the form of orbs in photographs or videos. Also, cold spots can be a sign of paranormal activity. We know from experience that many times if there's paranormal activity, it will be cold in the area of the activity. The temperature will change in a particular spot we've been dealing with during an investigation. We've gone into houses where one room will be 20° colder than another room. There is no heater or air conditioning running. It is not a case of poor insulation, and it is not due to a draft.

A pet reaction is also something that can alert you to danger. I have a boxer named Bubba, and he is sensitive to things. Sometimes we will hear something outside, and he will look at me as if to say, "Did you hear that too?" Pets sometimes have a different ability to sense things. I have had people send me videos of their animals growling at something that the humans cannot see. Animals are sometimes afraid to go down a certain hall or resist going to certain places in a home.

We've also worked cases where the demons hate the animals. They will absolutely kill some animals because these animals are exposing them. Protective animals can become enemies to demons. We had a case in Van Buren, Arkansas, where two witnesses saw a cat violently thrown against a wall and be killed.

Individuals suddenly crave different foods, and they eat foods they used to hate but now they can't get enough of them. Different personalities and voices can absolutely be a sure sign that there is something going on with a person. When we are doing our investigation and trying to figure things out, we want to know if the person has mental illness or if a person is experiencing true paranormal activity. This oftentimes comes up, and people see different personalities and hear different voices. We've worked many exorcisms where the demons talk, and they will often talk to us.

When we talk to them, we discover that they have different voices and personalities than the person they're in. In fact, they override oftentimes the will of the person. It's very important that you understand that there is a difference between a believer and an unbeliever when it comes to how a demon can work in them. If there is a demon, that demon must have permission to be there. He must be assigned to that person by Satan. Many times, the demon knows that person better than themselves. They've studied them and watched them, and they see what upsets them. They see what makes them laugh; they watch their hidden sins to see what they're drawn to, and then that's what they use as temptation to draw them. They eventually open up a portal so that they can come in and take control.

Many people report seeing apparitions and ghosts. I'm fine whether you believe in ghosts or if you choose not to believe in ghosts. I think it's demons and not ghosts most of the time. Most people that study this will tell you that ghosts have the same traits and personalities after they've died. If they were nice in their life before they died, their ghost will probably be nice. If they are angry, bitter, or dangerous, then I would say they're evil. When we do deliverance and exorcisms, we don't say, "If you're a ghost, it's okay to stay here as long as you're good." In fact, we've had people turn down our ministry because they'll say we want you to get rid of some of the spirits but not all the spirits. If they say, "We want you to get rid of some of the ghosts— just the bad ones," we say no. If we come in, we clean and remove everything that's not human. We are getting rid of all spirits. We are not going to take that risk. Let me just warn you: something can pretend to be good in the spirit world and seem to have good intentions, but they are evil. We are not going to take a chance, and I encourage you, if you're reading this, to not play around with it.

Another thing you should not play around with is magic. It can lead to paranormal activity. There is no good magic. People will claim they will just practice good magic. They claim to have good motives, and they may claim to draw on the positive energy of the universe and the earth. But it ties into supernatural powers. It can start off good and fun, but then the devil and his demons come in to tempt you to get in deeper. They are not going to give you their full agenda. It's kind of like when people just meet. If I ask, "How long have you been dating?" and they reply, "about 3 weeks," and they think they know everything about each other. Well, first the dating era is something I call the "cover up." That's when you're hiding everything bad in your life. The same is true in the world of magic. There may be a Wicca group that will offer friendship, intrigue, and witchcraft. There are demonic forces working behind the scenes to cover up their real agenda, which sometimes leads to darker magic, curses, and death.

The bottom line is that every demon wants to kill you. There are distinct kinds of demons. There are suicide demons, but there are also death demons, and they absolutely want you dead.

Another common thing that happens to people is a feeling of being pinned down. We were in Oklahoma recently, and when we entered the living room, they showed us a particular couch. This person had been pinned down there by a demon and could not move. I have personally experienced this. When I was in college, I was preparing to be an Arkansas State trooper. This was before I was called to the ministry. I came in late one night and laid down on the couch. All of a sudden, I felt a presence overtake me, and it pushed me down. I felt something heavy on me, and I wanted it to get off, but I had no strength. I had no ability to push it off. I couldn't even talk, and I kept looking over at the light switch because I wanted to turn the lights on. Something in me knew they wouldn't like the light. All I could do in my mind was say Jesus. Jesus helped me, and after a few moments of saying Jesus in my mind, it departed. When it left me, I felt it lift off me literally. I turned the lights on and stayed up late that night. About twenty percent of people experience sleep paralysis occasionally. It is a state of temporarily feeling paralyzed when falling asleep or waking up. The scientific explanation for it is that the brain is misinterpreting sensory input. In a majority of these episodes, the sleeper has a hallucination. It can be influenced by their culture or beliefs. Many people report seeing demons, malevolent figures, or shadow figures in the room. People say they can't talk, and many try to speak but cannot. Many people say they struggle to say the name of Jesus, and that as soon as they can say it out loud, the feeling lifts.

Another sign that someone is under demonic influence is that they can't tolerate church or praise music. Many don't want to go to church, and they criticize everything and everyone at church. Some people are especially offended by communion. If your kids, husband or wife, or somebody you're working with cannot tolerate these things, then that is a sign to which you should pay attention. The enemy hates praise music. Music can influence our moods and our minds. Many times, demons will use music to stream bad words, suicidal thoughts, and rebellious ideas into our minds.

If you are trying to figure out how to discern paranormal activity, it is important to know some signs to look for. For example, you might notice things like an unexplained knowledge of history or a sudden ability to speak another language. Those are clear signs. For example, if a 12-year-old can suddenly speak three languages he never learned, that is a sign of demonic possession. A demon has been around a long time and has knowledge that the person themselves never learned.

We have been doing exorcisms on multiple cases where, when we start reading scripture, the demon will ask, "Would you like for us to read that back to you in Latin?" Demons are very smart, and they have been around a long time. They were created originally as angels with personalities, and they're very smart. They know history, they know languages, and some of them claim they can predict future events. I've had many people that I've worked with say that their demons will tell them things that are going to happen in the future. How far into the future and how accurate, we are not for sure. The people will say that the demon told them this guy's going to do this to you, or this girl's going to say this to you, or your boss is going to fire you tomorrow, or you're going to get a raise tomorrow. It happens, and it can be coincidental, but some of it can be assigned.

Another very common sign of paranormal activity is when the whole family is afraid to sleep in their own rooms. We should especially pay close attention to our children. Sometimes kids don't want to go to bed, and sometimes that's because they want to stay up and play games or watch TV. That’s one thing. But it's totally different if they're afraid to go into the room and go to bed. Please wise up and believe your children if they're afraid of a certain closet, for example. Janie and I will tell you that we have experienced demons in closets. We also experience them in basements and in attics. When we go into a home to do a cleansing or an exorcism, these demons will move around. We usually have three on our team, and it's interesting as we work. Sometimes, we'll separate when we're moving around in the house. One time my adopted daughter and I were working on a case of a young teenage boy. We knew there was something demonic in the house. We were trying to discover where it was, and she came and got me, and she said it's under the bed in the bedroom. As soon as I walked in the door, there was a reaction. I knew immediately that the child was correct. Sometimes kids and adults have a unique sensitivity. They are sensitive, and they have good discernment about spiritual things. Then there are some people that can sit down and eat dinner with a possessed person and not even sense that anything is wrong. There are other people that can detect something paranormal, like a demon or ghost, very easily. There have been many times that others have pointed out things to me that I needed to see. That's been very helpful.

It's not as easy as you might think to go in and do a cleansing or an exorcism. You must figure out what is there, why it is there, who gave it permission to be there, and what its purpose is. I will just be honest and say here that I think our team is excellent at doing this. We are effective. People have expressed that their lives have been saved.

Some people say that by coming to their home, we rescued them because the paranormal activity was so bad. We have gone into homes many times where the activity is so powerful and so strong that the parents and all the kids have moved out of their bedrooms and they're sleeping in the living room on the couch together. Or they make a pallet in the living room because they're afraid to go to their own rooms. This is heartbreaking. We, as a team, believe that we have been called by God. We believe that God has given us power and anointing to fight these things.

We have been called to help when a child is showing violent behavior. We see cases where the children suddenly want to kill their pets and cut off baby dolls' heads. We went to a home where an older girl had taken all her baby dolls, beheaded them, and had the heads hanging on a clothesline in the room.

In another case, a young family bought a home, and they discovered a pentagram had been placed in the basement. There were also at least 100 plastic skulls that resembled human skulls in different places in the house. One of the neighbors reported that the guy that lived there was called the skull man, and he was very evil. In fact, he was in prison because he had kidnapped and raped many kids, some probably even in that very house that we were cleansing. Pay attention to dark items that focus on death or satanic symbols when you go into a home. We have found weird kinds of writing on the wall. Sometimes there are hidden pentagrams in places, especially in older homes. Sometimes there is negative energy from people that lived there before or events that had happened there. Demons and ghosts may be attached to these homes because they're comfortable there. They mark that home. Many times, when we go in to help, the first thing the demon will say to us is "Hey you, get out of this house." Of course, they don't use clean language. Demons do not mind cursing. Everything about them is filthy and dirty. Remember that paranormal activity is to be taken seriously; it's not a joke. It's not something to play with, and it can really create problems.

Often, the first thing the demon will say to us is that these people want us here and they do not want us to leave. I say to never open a portal by consulting a medium. Practicing witchcraft has also become very common. The Wicca movement is very powerful in America, and it is affecting a lot of younger people in their twenties and thirties.

Instead of accepting the mainline Christian or Catholic religions, today they're choosing the dark side and playing with magic spells and the Ouija board.

I can give you several examples where something has been cursed or it has a demonic attachment. It could be a bracelet, a necklace of crystals, an idol, items used in rituals, or many other things like antiques. You may ask, "Well, why in the world would a demon be attached to an object that is nonliving?" Because if you bring an object into your home and they are attached to it, then demons feel that gives them permission to come to your home. A curse can be very serious, and it doesn't have to be something that's 100 years old bought at an antique store. Someone evil could work in a factory somewhere, and they could be putting curses on everything they touch down the assembly line. I would encourage you to bless everything that comes into your house. If you buy something new, pray over it, bless it, and give it to God.

I want to mention a case in Greenwood, Arkansas, where our office is located. A lady came to see me one morning at the office, and she brought in a huge family Bible. It had a black, eerie cover. The Bible was probably printed in the early 1900s; it appeared to be well over 100 years old. She said, "I heard who you were, and I heard you were a paranormal pastor, so I wanted to come and talk to you. My brother, who has been into drugs and alcohol, found this Bible in his home. He doesn't even know how it got there. And she said when he showed it to me, I said there's something wrong with that Bible. I prayed about it, and I realized then that any object can be cursed, even a Bible." That was an eye-opening experience for us.

We're getting more and more people that are calling us to come in and do house blessings and even business blessings. We performed a blessing on a large dentist office in Corpus Christi, Texas, and when we got there, we discovered that a man had killed himself in the building, and there have been several deaths in that place since.

We were called to an antique store in Arkansas. It was a really serious case where one of the employees there had bought a candle holder and a jewelry box from a certain booth within the store. The owner purchased these two items from the rented booth space and took the candleholder and jewelry box home. She said bad things immediately started happening in her house. Her four-year-old son had a terrible dream where he saw a demon come into the window of the house.

He mentioned the shop that they had bought it and that the demon/monster was tied to the shop. She said they were all sick the next day. They were projectile vomiting, and she realized she needed to start praying. God revealed to her that those two objects, the candleholder and jewelry box, were evil, and they needed to be taken out of the house immediately. When she went back to the store to the area where she had bought those, we found that there were all kinds of notes about rituals. They found out that the candle holder had been used in a ritual, and there were several other evil items for sale in that booth area. The items were removed out of the store, and we did a full cleansing of the store, which took several hours.

I hope that this chapter has made you aware that paranormal activity is real and to be aware of things around you. If things are going on in your house or business, don't rule out that it might be paranormal activity.

Col 1:12-14 says, "Giving thanks unto the Father, which hath made us meet to be partakers of the inheritance of the saints in light: Who hath delivered us from the power of darkness, and hath translated us into the kingdom of his dear Son, in whom we have redemption through his blood, even the forgiveness of sins."

This scripture is one of our theme verses that we use for Telling the Truth Ministry. The reason I think this scripture is fitting here is that it points out that people can be delivered from the power of darkness. If you are experiencing any of the signs of paranormal activity that come from darkness, you can get help. You can experience victory and live an abundant life!

*Chapter 8*

# Is Mental Illness Disguising Demonic Activity?

One of the biggest challenges surrounding deliverance ministries is the confusion between mental illness and authentic demonic activity. Determining whether someone is mentally ill or possibly influenced by demons is a complex matter and often requires professional expertise. It is possible for a demon-possessed person or oppressed person to visit a psychiatrist or psychologist and behave perfectly normal. On the other hand, evil spirits can also disguise themselves as a symptom of a mental illness.

Richard Gallagher put it this way:

> Evil spirits can consciously mimic genuine illnesses or disorders to disguise or mask their presence. Such counterfeit cases are often confused with psychiatric disorders because their symptoms, including trances and altered states of consciousness, often overlap. Evil spirits try to stimulate further confusion by adding other less dramatic symptoms, most notably states of pain, generalized trembling, and other manifestations. Demons are not stupid, and they love to confuse people, perhaps particularly members of the clergy and medical professions. What better way than to disguise their nefarious activities as a human malady? (Gallagher, 2020, p. 113)

There is frequently a conflict between the opinions of clergy who conduct deliverances or exorcisms and the doctors and those from secular fields. In my experience, psychologists and psychiatrists as a group seem to be less religious than most people in the population of America. In the past, many of them have tended to not consider the possibility of demonic activity. However, currently there is a trend for many of these individuals to take into consideration the beliefs and superstitions of their patients. A few therapists are even willing to consider letting a priest or pastor help with treatment. They might say there is the possibility of a benefit to their patient because of a type of placebo effect.

> Ragan, Maloney & Beit-Hallahmi (1976), in a more recent study of members of the American Psychological Association reported that 43% of the sample stated a belief in a transcendent deity, 47% were members or were at least infrequent attenders of a religious institution, and 27% attended half the time or more. These findings support the perception that psychologists as a group are less religious as compared to the general population, as reported by Ragan et al. (1976); however, the results do not support the popular contention that psychologists, in toto, are irreligious or anti- religious. (Shafranske & Gorsuch, 1984, pp. 231-232)

However, in recent times, there has been more of an openness to supernatural phenomena that relate to the suffering of people. I believe this is true because there are so many cases where administering medication or using traditional therapy has not worked. I know that in my ministry, I am receiving more referrals from doctors and psychiatrists than ever before. Let me be clear: not all therapists, counselors, psychologists, and psychiatrists are closed-minded to the possibilities of demonic influence being a factor in people's struggles. I have had several of these individuals in the megachurches where I pastored, and they have reached out to me for help with some of their patients at times.

The debate between mental illness only versus demonic influence has also produced controversy between many different denominations. There are a wide variety of opinions.

> Mercer added that among Charismatic Christians (not all of whom are Pentecostals), opinion varies about the need for psychological or psychiatric training or other education for people working with individuals with mental illness. Anglicans and Roman Catholics make deliverance the task of ordained clergy people and expect them to consider psychological and psychiatric concepts before taking a supernatural approach. Pentecostals, however, generally have little hierarchical organization. In addition, although Pentecostals may use psychological terms and concepts, they do not consider professional treatment essential for casting out demons, nor do they think people require any ordination or training. (Parks, p. 101)

The Southern Baptist Convention is one of the largest Christian denominations in the United States of America. As a Southern Baptist pastor who served in key leadership positions in the Southern Baptist Convention for over forty years, I can attest to the fact that many of them primarily assign all of these behaviors as mental illness and ignore the possibility of demonic possession or influences. Even though most of their pastors believe that the devil and demons attack people today, they would not be favorable toward deliverance ministries or exorcisms. Some of their pastors believe that a person can get rid of their own demons without any assistance from others. I am thankful that more of them are beginning to realize the value of deliverance ministries.

Jean Mercer, author of *Deliverance, Demonic Possession, and Mental Illness,* points out:

In the Western world, mainstream Christians and Jews generally consider natural factors in mental illness and mental health interventions despite their acknowledgment of the importance of spiritual or supernatural phenomena.Pentecostal believers, on the other hand, emphasize the role of the supernatural in both the causation and healing of mental and physical disorders. Pentecostals believe these disorders result from demonic possession. (Mercer, 2013)

Cultures all over the world have reported occurrences of possession. Many people from Africa, South America, India, and China admit the reality that demonic possession and oppression are possible.

"Much of the world is mystified by the West's refusal to acknowledge the existence of spirits and takes a dim view of any therapy that excludes spiritual healing from the picture." (Stafford, 2005, p. 25)

It is my opinion that there are people who have mental illness. They may have a history of mental illness in their family. Almost everyone has at least one person in their family that suffers from mental illness. They may have a chemical imbalance. Medication can help their symptoms. However, let me be clear. I believe that in many cases, Satan and his demons are using mental illness as a disguise to attack individuals. If people assume that someone is just mentally'ill, they will not encourage them to get any spiritual help. If a demon is present, he will have free reign in that person's life. We must be honest that mental illness and demonic activity are both real. In many cases, we have found that a person can have both. In fact, mental illness can open portals for demonic attacks. Demons are bullies and will often attack people who are vulnerable. Likewise, demonic activity can also cause mental illness. We talk to lots of people who have been afraid to tell anyone what is happening because they are afraid people will think they are crazy.

Here are some things to consider if you suspect someone may have mental illness.

1. Behavioral Signs: Look for unusual or disruptive behavior that deviates significantly from the person's usual conduct.
2. Emotional State: Note extreme emotions or mood swings that are not typical for the person.
3. Cognitive Functioning: Assess their ability to think clearly, reason, and communicate effectively.
4. Physical Symptoms: Check for any physical symptoms that might accompany certain mental disorders. They may have a chemical imbalance or a traumatic brain injury. They may have been prescribed medicine by a doctor. People who know them would say that the medicine helps if they take it properly. Find out if the person has had a traumatic brain injury.
5. Duration: Consider the duration and persistence of the symptoms—mental illnesses often have a continuous impact on daily life.
6. Context: Evaluate the person's life circumstances, stressors, and any history of mental health issues in their family.

These are some general descriptions and symptoms of common mental illnesses. It's important to note that each person's experience with a mental disorder can vary, and diagnosis should be made by qualified mental health professionals based on comprehensive evaluation and assessment of symptoms and their impact on daily life. This is a list of some of the most common mental illnesses, along with brief definitions and typical symptoms associated with each:

### 1. Depression (Major Depressive Disorder)

*Definition:*

Depression is a mood disorder characterized by persistent sadness, loss of interest or pleasure in activities, and other symptoms that affect daily functioning.

*Symptoms:*

- Persistent sad, anxious, or "empty" mood
- Feelings of hopelessness or pessimism
- Loss of interest or pleasure in hobbies and activities
- Fatigue or decreased energy
- Difficulty concentrating, remembering details, and making decisions
- Insomnia or excessive sleeping
- Changes in appetite or weight
- Thoughts of death or suicide, suicide attempts

Demons like to steal people's joy. There definitely are suicide demons. However, depression can be normal in certain life situations. Demons can cause night terrors or nightmares that cause people to not sleep well. If someone is having thoughts of suicide, inquire to see if they are "hearing" messages in their heads. Demons will lie to people and will pretend to be dead souls, angels, or some deity. They may claim to be a spiritual guide or a protector.

### 2. Anxiety Disorders

*Definition:*

Anxiety disorders involve excessive fear or anxiety and are the most common mental disorders in the United States.

*Symptoms (vary depending on specific anxiety disorder):*

- Excessive worry and apprehension
- Restlessness or feeling on edge
- Fatigue
- Difficulty concentrating or mind going blank
- Irritability
- Muscle tension
- Sleep disturbances (difficulty falling or staying asleep, or restless, unsatisfying sleep)
- Panic attacks (sudden onset of intense fear or discomfort, often accompanied by physical symptoms like rapid heartbeat, sweating, trembling, and shortness of breath)

Demons like to cause fear. Many families who call us are so scared in their own homes that they are all sleeping in one room together.

Many demonic situations could cause anxiety.

## 3. Bipolar Disorder

*Definition:*

Bipolar disorder, formerly known as manic-depressive illness, is a mood disorder characterized by extreme mood swings that include emotional highs (mania or hypomania) and lows (depression).

*Symptoms:*

- Manic episode: elevated mood, increased energy, racing thoughts, decreased need for sleep, excessive involvement in

pleasurable activities with a high risk of negative consequences
- Hypomanic episode (less severe form of mania)
- Major depressive episode (as described in depression)

People with bipolar disorder should remain under a doctor's care. I would encourage them to continue taking their medicine.

## 4. Schizophrenia

*Definition:*

Schizophrenia is a chronic and severe mental disorder that affects how a person thinks, feels, and behaves. It often involves distorted thinking, hallucinations, and reduced ability to function.

*Symptoms:*

- Delusions (false beliefs)
- Hallucinations (seeing or hearing things that others do not)
- Disorganized thinking (incoherent or illogical thoughts)
- Disorganized or abnormal motor behavior (e.g., catatonia)
- Negative symptoms (reduced emotional expression, difficulty starting and sustaining activities)

It is possible that some people who are under demonic influence could be listening to the lies of the devil and have false beliefs and delusions. Some people who have been seeing and hearing things in their homes could be misdiagnosed because some psychiatrists think they are hallucinating.

Francis MacNutt shares this story about a woman who was misdiagnosed.

I once prayed for a young woman who had been confined in a mental hospital for twelve years, suffering from schizophrenia.

After two hours of prayer for healing and deliverance, the glazed look in her eyes left, and she was able to converse in a normal way. Several weeks later, the doctors recognized a dramatic change in her behavior and released her from the hospital. I could cite many more examples from a steady stream of supplicants . . . unable to find help from psychotherapy or from those who are ministers of religion who had not learned to deal with the demonic. (MacNutt, 1995, p. 23)

## 5. Post-Traumatic Stress Disorder (PTSD)

*Definition:*

PTSD can develop after exposure to a traumatic event and is characterized by symptoms such as intrusive memories, avoidance of reminders of the event, negative changes in thinking and mood, and hyperarousal.

*Symptoms:*

- Intrusive memories (flashbacks, distressing dreams)
- Avoidance of reminders of the traumatic event
- Negative changes in mood and thinking
- Hyperarousal (easily startled, feeling tense or on edge, difficulty sleeping)

Demons can sometimes take advantage of a traumatic event to find a reason to attach to someone. For example, people may become bitter and unforgiving. Unforgiveness is a common portal used by demons. Demons can also cause bad dreams. If someone is experiencing paranormal situations, it can cause them to feel tense or on edge.

## 6. Borderline Personality Disorder (BPD)

*Definition:*

BPD is a mental health disorder characterized by unstable moods, behaviors, and relationships. Individuals with BPD often have intense fears of abandonment, unstable self-image, and impulsive behavior.

*Symptoms:*

- Intense fear of abandonment
- Unstable relationships (idealization and devaluation of others)
- Unstable self-image or sense of self
- Impulsive and risky behavior (e.g., substance abuse, reckless driving, unsafe sex)
- Emotional instability (rapid mood swings, intense anger, depression)

People who are possessed or being influenced may appear unstable. It is possible for demons to cause strife and confusion in relationships, thereby destabilizing them. Demons can specialize and attack people in various ways. For example, there are demons of addiction. Some demons tempt people to do risky behavior.

## 7. Dissociative Identity Disorder (DID) formerly known as Multiple Personality Disorder

*Definition:*

Dissociative identity disorder (DID) is a dissociative disorder where two or more distinct personality states or identities alternate in controlling the person's behavior. Each identity may have its own distinct way of thinking, feeling, and relating to others.

*Symptoms:*

1. Presence of Multiple Identities: the presence of two or more distinct personality states or identities, each with its own way of interacting and experiencing the world. These identities may have different names, personal histories, mannerisms, and even physiological responses.
2. Amnesia: gaps in memory that are more extensive than normal forgetfulness. These gaps can affect personal information, everyday events, or traumatic events.
3. Identity disturbances: significant disruption in the person's sense of self and identity. This may include feeling disconnected from oneself or one's surroundings.
4. Depersonalization: feeling detached from one's body, thoughts, or sensations. This can manifest as feeling like an outside observer of oneself.
5. Derealization: A sense of unreality about one's surroundings or the world. The environment may seem distorted, dreamlike, or unfamiliar.
6. Severe Stress or Trauma: Typically, DID is associated with a history of severe trauma, often occurring in childhood, such as physical, sexual, or emotional abuse.
7. Functional Impairment: The presence of these symptoms must cause significant distress or impairment in social, occupational, or other important areas of functioning.

It's important to note that DID is a controversial and complex diagnosis, and it requires careful evaluation by mental health professionals experienced in dissociative disorders. Treatment often involves psychotherapy, particularly approaches that focus on integrating different identities and addressing underlying trauma.

Out of all the possible diagnoses listed above, this is the one that is most like possession. Psychiatrist M. Scott Peck, M.D. put it this way.

The currently recognized disorder that manifests symptoms most like possession is Multiple Personality Disorder, or MPD (currently labeled and diagnosed as dissociative identity disorder). Only in the past few years has MPD itself come under serious question as a valid diagnosis. (Peck M. S., 2005, p. 101)

Dissociative Identity Disorder (formerly Multiple Personality Disorder) and spirit oppression or possession have some differences.

Psychiatrists frequently refer to Occam's razor, which indicates that the simplest explanation—that is, the solution that requires the fewest assumptions—is preferable.

Occam's Razor is a sound principle, and MPD is often the correct diagnosis when bizarre behavior bearing no relation to a patient's basic personality suddenly turns up. But MPD does not account for all the relevant data here.

First, in MPD the core personality, according to Peck, "is virtually always unaware of the existence of the secondary personalities—at least until close to the very end of prolonged, successful treatment." But in cases of spirit oppression, patients are "either aware from the beginning or [are] readily made aware not only of the self-destructive part of them but also that this part [has] a distinct and alien personality" (Peck M. S., 1983, pp. 192-193). Second, trying to cast out an alter is, according to MacNutt, "an impossible task since these alters are mostly fragments of the person's personality" (MacNutt, 1995, p. 231). Yet casting out an oppressing spirit is not only possible but likely when the necessary expertise is available. (Stafford, 2005, p. 23)

There are indeed people that are under demonic influence. There is a wide variety of ways that people can be oppressed, possessed, vexed, or influenced. This is another way that demons can cause confusion. Here are some things to consider.

1. *Behavioral Signs:* The person may report seeing or hearing things that are paranormal, such as poltergeist activity. For example, the cabinet doors may open and shut, windows can slam, and things can be moved with no explanation. They may be drawn to dark things. For example, they may have been dabbling in witchcraft, playing with tarot cards or a Ouija Board, worshiping Satan, etc. They may do things that are out of their normal character.

2. *Emotional State:* They become negative toward anything religious. Discussions about religion may be met with scorn or anger. They may be terrified by the things they have been seeing and hearing. They may be embarrassed to tell anyone. They may feel stressed.

3. *Cognitive Functioning:* They may be especially fascinated with dark things. For example, they may research New Age or eastern philosophy. They may read books on witchcraft, wicca, or Satan. They may have knowledge that is beyond their education. They might sometimes speak in a language that they never learned. They may use the pronoun "we" when talking to them. There can be many demons assigned to an individual.

4. *Physical symptoms:* They may have marks on their bodies that are not self-inflicted or from another person. They may desire foods that they never liked before. They may be tired from lack of sleep. People may smell something strange.

They may feel and see the blankets being pulled off them in bed, for example.

5. *Reaction to Religious Items or Places:* When shown a cross, they may look at it with disgust. Many times, they will try to turn a cross upside down or throw it across the room. We worked with a young girl in Corpus Christi, Texas, once who became physically ill when she came into the church building. She told us, "I always get sick if I enter a church." She turned around and left without getting help.

6. *Reaction to Rituals or Prayer:* They may refuse to let anyone pray over them or participate in a religious ritual. Often when I begin to pray over someone, I see a physical reaction if there are demonic influences present. For example, after an exorcism, some priests will have the person take communion as a test to see if they get a negative reaction. Demons do not like the idea of the blood of Christ.

7. *Corroboration:* In many cases, friends or family have seen and heard things or seen evidence of strange occurrences or behavior. There have been many times when a parent has brought their child to us, saying that they believe their child is possessed or being attacked by demons. Sometimes paranormal investigators verify that there is evidence of paranormal activity. Some psychiatrists, having no success with counseling, psychotherapy, or medication, will request assistance from a spiritual source.

8. *Exclusion of Mental Illness:* Before considering spiritual causes, mental health professionals should first rule out mental illness or other medical explanations. If a person is on medication, we highly recommend that they stay on their medicine.

Alton Parks, in his thesis for Liberty University, makes the following interesting point:

> In addition, there are instances when mental illness and demonic possession occur at the same time. Many times, clergy face a fine line in discerning if a person is demonically possessed or has a mental illness. Most mental illnesses are the result of chemical imbalances or traumatic experiences.

Chemical imbalances do not indicate anything demonic; however, some traumatic events are connected to demonic activity, which is why there is such a fine line between mental illness and demonic possession. (Parks, 2020)

We have found that traumatic events can open a door that allows the demons to enter. They can cause hatred, bitterness, and unforgiveness. They can also cause depression and feelings so overwhelming that it could bring out thoughts of hopelessness and suicide.

Richard Gallagher, a Princeton University graduate, trained at Yale in psychiatry. He is a psychiatrist who has been investigating possession and demonic attacks for twenty-five years. He shares this story about a girl named Sara.

> She may have been targeted because of her sheer goodness and devotion to God and others. She certainly felt 'attacked', or at least strongly 'bothered' in her view, and was undergoing weird but non-psychiatric symptoms, apparently paranormal in nature. Her odd state was not happening, it seemed, because she had turned to evil or unsavory occult practices; she denied any of those factors in her background. (Gallagher, 2020, p. 95)

I would like to point out that demonic attack is not always a result of people delving into sinful lifestyles, being cursed, or doing something that would open them up to demonic influence. Demons are often assigned to bring down a pastor, priest, or strong Christian leader.

They will try to damage their reputation. Their health may be attacked. They will tempt them, harass them, and try to hinder these people from doing God's work.

A few interesting points are made by Richard Gallagher, M.D. He reminds us that it is possible for a mentally ill person to claim to be possessed to get attention.

> There are disturbed patients who merely pretend to suffer from various dramatic psychological or medical conditions, and even individuals who historically have feigned possession. But I believe these latter cases are rare. The possibility of an outright pretense, rather, is a condition better characterized as a 'factitious disorder', where a patient makes a conscious effort to mislead others out of various motives, including a desire to be in the spotlight. (Gallagher, 2020, p. 111)

Demons can mimic medical conditions. Both physicians and spiritual leaders need to be aware that demons try to hide behind medical diagnoses in order to prevent the person from getting the spiritual help that they really need.

> Physicians and exorcists are working to the same end of helping suffering individuals. Not all exorcists need to know everything about medicine, and not all physicians need to believe in the reality of demonic conditions to assist exorcists. What they must be willing to do, however, is to approach their respective tasks of discernment with a spirit of humility and collaboration. ...They best assist by ensuring that no medical pathology explains the phenomena in question, leaving open the possibility that something potentially paranormal might be happening. This critical role on their part can save all parties an enormous amount of time and effort by ruling out from the start

> conditions that only mimic diabolic conditions. The tendency for demonic states to imitate medical conditions is the critical point here—and, in my view, is no accident." (Gallagher, 2020, p. 113)

In summary, determining whether someone is mentally ill, possessed, or possibly influenced by demons requires careful observation, consideration of many factors, and often involves input from trained professionals in both mental health and spiritual guidance. It's crucial to approach these situations with sensitivity, respect, and a commitment to finding the best possible care for the individual.

# Chapter 8 Resources

Gallagher, R. M. (2020). *Demonic Foes: My Twenty-five Years as a Psychiatrist Investigating Possessions, Diabolic Attacks, and the Paranormal.* New York, NY: Harper One.

MacNutt, F. (1995). *Deliverance from Evil Spirits.* Grand Rapids, MI: Chosen Books.

Mercer, J. (2013). Deliverance, Demonic Possession, and Mental Illness: Some Considerations for Mental Health Professionals. *Mental Health, Religion & Culture 16, no. 6,* 595.

Parks, A. (2020). *Mental Illness and Demonic Influence: The Difference Between Them and the Difference It Makes.* in Candidacy for the degree of Doctor of Ministry: A Thesis Project Submitted to the Faculty of Liberty University School of Divinity.

Peck, M. S. (1983). *People of the Lie.* New York, NY: Simon & Schuster. Peck, M. S. (2005). *Glimpses of the Devil: A Psychiatrist's Personal*

*Accounts of Possession, Exorcism, and Redemption.* New York, NY: Free Press, a Division of Simon & Schuster, Inc.

Shafranske, E., & Gorsuch, R. (1984). Factors Associated with Perceptions of Spirituality and Psychotherapy. *Journal of Transpersonal Psychology 16,* 231-241.

Stafford, B. (2005). The Growing Evidence for Demonic Possession: What Should Psychiatry's Response Be? *Journal of Religion and Health 44, no. 1,* 13-30.

*Chapter 9*

# How To Do an Effective Exorcism and Deliverance

When we talk about exorcisms, we mean to exorcize or to cast out. Some people feel they need a pastor to help with exorcisms, and there are a lot of individuals that have different backgrounds and differing opinions about whether exorcisms really work. I think it is a fair question to ask. The Catholic Church refers to casting out demons as exorcisms. Most Protestant churches use the word deliverance, but they mean the same thing. Deliverance is the process of getting rid of evil spirits or getting demons out of someone's life.

When deliverance is needed, some uninformed preacher might tell you that all demons are the same. I will say that in my movement, the Protestant movement, there is a lot of skepticism toward exorcisms and deliverances. They have a lot of doubts and wonder if they work. If you interview pastors, many will tell you they don't have much experience dealing with this. I am friends with a megachurch pastor in Texas who's a great pastor, but he does not have a good understanding of the issue of deliverance and exorcism. I don't hold this against him; he is representative of many pastors who have not been taught how to deal with demonic issues. I hope this book will open the eyes of many to see the reality of demons.

Christians can have a single demon or multiple demons in their life. There are a lot of people who say that if someone is a born-again

Christian, they don't have to worry about demons in their life. There's a Greek word for that, and it's called baloney. I've heard people say,

"Well, my pastor said that if I'm a Christian, I don't have to worry about demons." That is absolutely not true. We need to understand there are different kinds of attachments, and then there's total possession, where someone is totally possessed by demons. Fully possessed people have demons that can take control over them. If someone is a true, born-again Christian, they cannot be demon possessed. The word possessed means ownership, and I believe that if you are saved, then you are owned by the Lord Jesus Christ. In other words, your soul today either belongs to the devil or it belongs to the Lord. Your soul is very important. That's why these demons come after us. They also affect our bodies physically and attach to us. Mentally, our mind can have demons attached to our thoughts. There are different levels. If you are a Christian, it is still possible to struggle with demons. You may not be demon-possessed, but you can be what we call demonized, and that is when demons influence you. There's not a whole lot of difference because if there are demons in your life, you're going to have problems. They will break down relationships; they will attack your mind, and they're going to cause you to become something you don't want to be.

To perform an effective deliverance or exorcism, first we start off by believing in the power of prayer. When we are contacted by someone who needs help, we start to pray, and we ask our prayer partners to start praying for the situation. When we pray, God moves against these dark entities. When we pray in the name of Jesus, the Lord hears us. Secondly, it comes down to believing the Bible and all the scriptures mentioned about delivering people from evil, unclean spirits. The Bible is filled with over 130 scriptures that tell us that God will help and there is hope if there are demons in your life.

Scripture tells us that demons are fallen angels. They are powerful, with many different levels of authority. We know there are many types of demons, such as: suicide, addiction, pornography, hindering, affliction, religious, strife, depression, confusion, fear, etc. Some demons are more violent than others. They will break up your marriage if they can and they will destroy your children. Demons love to destroy all relationships, but the number one thing they want to destroy is your relationship with God. Your relationship with God is the most important relationship any person can have, and destroying that is their number one goal. Many Christians believe they can defeat demons on their own, but sometimes help is needed. When there is a team of people working together, there is strength. When there are more links in the chain, it does nothing but make us all stronger. The Bible tells us in these three scriptures, Matthew 10:1, Luke 9:1, and Mark 6:7. In Matthew 10:1 it says, "And he called his twelve disciples; he gave them power against unclean spirits, to cast them out, and to heal all manner of sickness and all manner of disease." The Bible says that a disciple is a follower of Jesus, and we are all disciples of him. Jesus gave us authority. When our team comes in to help cleanse a house or cast out a demon, we have been given the authority by Jesus as stated in scripture.

Sometimes a house needs an exorcism, or a property needs cleansing. We do what we call a prayer walk. We traveled to Bakersfield, California, and did a prayer walk. We were in a very crime-ridden, evil part of Bakersfield. When we returned to Bakersfield after cleansing and deliverances, people told us there had been a tremendous difference since we came in and did the prayer walk against darkness. Jesus says in Matthew 10, and he gave them authority over these spirits to cast them out and to heal these diseases. Luke 9:1 says, "Then he called the twelve disciples together and gave them power and authority over all devils and to cure diseases." There's that word authority again; when we come to pray over you, we take authority.

When an exorcism has happened, we, by the authority of Jesus Christ, have commanded those demons, those evil spirits, to depart and to be taken away. Jesus has called us his disciples and, together, has given us authority over all demons. There is one more scripture in

Mark 6:7 that says, "Calling the twelve to Him, he began to send them out two by two and gave them authority over impure spirits." If you have Jesus in your life, you proclaim to be a Christian, and you are a follower of Jesus, then you are his disciple.

Sometimes people wonder if it is biblical for a ministry team to go help. I heard a pastor in a large megachurch say, "You don't need a ministry team to come. You don't need help to have an exorcism." He's a good man, but, oh, he is so wrong. I've even had people call us names like the Ghostbusters of Texas, Kansas, and Arkansas. Some of the very people that have made fun of us have ended up calling me for help. Several pastors have commented that they've always believed but have never experienced it. We make no apologies for believing deliverances work in the power of Jesus' name. Based on the biblical worldview, true deliverance only comes with the help of Jesus and his name.

Many other religions practice exorcisms, but we believe that there are no true exorcisms where demons are made to leave and sent back to Hell without the power of God. We believe that it takes Jesus Christ and his blood. The power of Jesus and the blood of Jesus Christ when Jesus Christ died on that cross for you is the only thing to save you from a demon. These demons hate Jesus, and they hate his blood. We have over 300 prayer warriors we call upon when we go into a deliverance, and the power of prayer works. We can't do a deliverance without people praying. If you need help, don't give up.

The devil doesn't have to win because there is power in the name of Jesus Christ.

House cleansing is also very important. People can take back their homes and businesses from the devil. The Bible teaches us that we can take back the ground that the enemy has stolen from us.

Sometimes I get asked if what we do matters because Satan is going to do whatever he wants to do in our lives anyway. He wants you to think he can win. John 10:10 says, "The thief comes only to steal and kill and destroy; I came that they may have life, and have it abundantly." The number one goal of demons and the devil is to get your soul, and they will kill you. This stuff is dangerous. It's also dangerous to be in a church or to be under somebody's teaching who doesn't believe in the power of the devil and what he is doing. These pastors and ministers are not fully equipping their congregations for battle.

Some say a Christian cannot be attacked by Satan. Being a Christian does not mean that Satan will leave you alone. Satan can never get your soul, but he's not going to leave you alone. He worries about your influence; he worries about the light that has been given to you through your relationship with Jesus Christ. Start getting involved in praying and helping people get rid of demons. You are protected in the Lord, and our lives were put here to be light in darkness. The Bible is very clear about that. When we do this ministry, we're taking light into very dark places.

In John 10:10, Jesus says, "The thief only comes to steal, kill, and destroy. I came that they may have life, and may have it abundantly." Satan tries to destroy you; he tries to put you down; and he tries to discourage you in any way he can. Ephesians 6:10–11 says, "Finally, my brethren are strong in the Lord and his power.

Put on the whole armor of God so that you may be able to stand against the wiles of

the devil." The devil uses traps, schemes, and trickery to try to steal our joy and peace, kill us, and destroy our families, relationships, and our witness. This is a key verse for building a Biblical basis for what we do as we go and do deliverances and exorcisms We go on behalf of the Lord Jesus Christ. We go with his anointing, we go with his power, and we go with his blessings.

Ephesians 6:12 says, "For we wrestle not against flesh and blood but against principalities and against powers against the rulers of

darkness of this world." This verse is saying that we are in a fight; the word wrestle means we fight. We wrestle not against flesh and blood but against principalities. Satan has power over the principalities and rulers of the darkness. Demons can do all kinds of things. They can walk through walls; they can make us sick. Demons can get into our bodies, get attached to us, and even control a person who is not a Christian. As a Christian, the devil cannot make you do anything, but he can surely give you temptation. He will entice you, and he'll try to make you do bad things and lead you into all kinds of different sins. I have heard people say, "Well, I think we ought to do the work of the Lord, and we ought to be disciples for the Lord," but then they will completely dismiss the idea of casting out demons.

If we are going to follow the example of Jesus and his disciples, remember that Jesus had them cast out demons. As I've said before, a third of the ministry of Jesus on this earth was fighting demons. Isn't it funny how some preachers will encourage you to follow the part of the Great Commission that talks about going out and telling the world about Jesus, and yet they will not emphasize the part about casting out demons? The Bible contains many examples that show us how to be victorious in our own lives and when fighting demons. Jesus would tell us that we need to be out helping people and making a difference in people's lives.

This chapter deals with the two topics of exorcisms and deliverance. Deliverance really works. I'm going to start off by giving a scriptural view of why we do this. I have been involved in hundreds of exorcisms, some that I would call minor exorcisms, and some that I would designate as major, depending on what is going on with the person who we're trying to set free. The word exorcism means to evict or remove demons or malevolent spirits from the person. I tend to use the word deliverance more than exorcism.

The word exorcism is a term that is associated with the Catholic Church. I am not a Catholic. I have many friends that are Catholic, and I personally believe that there will be many Catholics in heaven, just like there will be people from many other denominations in heaven. But I'm a Protestant. I've been an active member of the Southern Baptist Church for nearly all my life. I've served as a Southern Baptist pastor. In some of the mainline denominations, there's kind of a stigma to the term exorcism, so I use the word deliverance. In fact, to be technical about it, deliverance is a type of healing. It is similar to a surgery where something needs to be removed or something needs to be repaired. It's a spiritual healing. You cannot have what I call a biblical exorcism or a biblical deliverance without a lot of prayer involved. And next to prayer is authority. You must have authority— those two things, prayer and authority, are essential. Not necessarily in that order, but both are involved. I want to talk about who can do an exorcism or deliverance because not everyone is willing and capable of doing one. I've heard some very well-meaning pastors say that anybody can do an exorcism. Anybody can take authority over a demon or demons. However, that simply is not factual.

We found that when we do deliverances and exorcisms, there's never just one demon. Generally, there's a group of demons. We find that there is what I call an alpha demon. This is the demon that is more powerful than the others and in charge of the mission. In our chapter on dealing with demons, we talk about the fact that not all demons are created the same. There are different kinds of demons, according to Ephesians chapter 6. When you talk about powers and principalities and you study the Greek language in which those were given to us from God himself, it lets us know that there are different levels of power in the spirit world. There are some demons that have different assignments. Every demon does have a specific assignment. And every demon is connected to Satan and responsible to Satan.

Demons are not only responsible to Satan; they also fear failing Satan by not accomplishing their task. Satan gives them an assignment and the power to do that assignment. In the scope of the spirit world, there are different demons and they have different abilities and different purposes. The passion and will of a demon to complete his task can affect the outcome of the deliverance.

Let me be clear and tell you that not only are deliverances biblical, they work. I John 3:8 talks about the son of God, Jesus, has come and was manifested. That word manifested literally means he was brought forth. Jesus was manifested to destroy the works of the devil, and that's what deliverance ministry is. It is through deliverance that we can destroy the works of the devil. How do the devil and his demons work? Well, they work through possessions and attachments. In the Bible, it talks about strongholds that are placed there in our lives. I believe that deliverance ministry and exorcisms do work when needed, and I think that the strongholds can be removed from our lives. You might say, "Well, that says that Jesus has come to destroy the works of the devil. That might work for Jesus, and I'm sure it did work for Jesus, but how can it work if Jesus is not here?" However, I would make the argument that Jesus is here! We are the instruments that Jesus uses today. We are the hands and feet of Jesus.

Let's be honest, the majority of the ministry on earth now since Jesus was resurrected and went to heaven is done through human beings. John 14:12 states, “Most assuredly, I say to you, he who believes in Me, the works that I do he will do also; and greater works than these he will do, because I go to My Father.” We have God’s power available to us through the person and power of the Holy Spirit.

When we are performing a deliverance for someone, we often invoke the Holy Trinity to enable us to defeat the dark ones that we are evicting. You cannot deny the power of the Holy Trinity and the fact that the Holy Trinity is very effective when it comes to exorcisms and deliverance. All three parts of the Trinity are used every time we do an exorcism because it's talking about God himself (God the father, God the Son, and God the Holy Spirit make up the Trinity.) In my many conversations with demons, they often resist and mock the Trinity. They hate the Holy Trinity. They will say to me that the Unholy Trinity is more powerful than the Holy Trinity. The Unholy Trinity consists of Satan instead of the heavenly Father, the antichrist instead of the Christ, and the false prophet instead of the Holy Spirit. The Unholy Trinity competes with the Holy Trinity. Every deliverance is a battle between good and evil.

There is no pastor or demonologist that can take on and do an exorcism and deliverance within their own power. The weakest demon with the lowest strength can defeat a human anytime.

Demons have power, and sometimes they can control people. Someone who's totally possessed is someone that's under complete control of Satan, and he has the power to make them do anything. They can make them say and do things. I think some of the horrific crimes that are committed today are done under the influence and control of Satan.

I saw the other day where a young girl and her boyfriend killed her mom and dad. They slaughtered them while they were in their bed. I can assure you that something that horrific has evil written all over it. When we do exorcisms and deliverances, we realize that it takes God's power to make the demons leave and set the person free.

They're stronger and more powerful than we are, but they're not more powerful than Jesus. Remember what it says in the scripture. Jesus was brought to us, and he was manifested to destroy the works of the devil. John 14:12 talks about when Jesus told his disciples that when he goes to heaven, when he dies on the cross and is resurrected, they were going to be able to do even greater works. He said he was going to empower them through the Holy Spirit to be able to do these works. Remember John 14:12 talking about the Kingdom work? Jesus came and was manifested to destroy the works of the devil, and we have been given his power and authority. I said as we started this chapter that it takes prayer and authority. To do an effective exorcism or deliverance, we must have authority.

Demons really want the person they're living in to die, and that is the bottom line. They want their soul, and they want to claim that soul for all eternity. We do these deliverances because it is spiritual healing for people who need to be delivered from these demons. The Bible says in John 10:10 that the enemy comes to kill and destroy, and we see the ministry as a rescue ministry. Some church members and even some pastors have referred to us in this ministry as special forces like in the military. In the military, we have the Army; the church, or the body of Christ, would be like the Army. And in the Army, you have a group of people who have been trained to be Special Forces and have different skills. Performing deliverances is an anointing. A person doesn't wake up someday and go out and become an exorcist or decide to be a demonologist. The call of God is allowing you to have training and has prepared you to be able to do so. In the Army, the special forces go in, and they tackle the most dangerous people, and they go behind enemy lines. That is what this ministry does with prayer and the authority given by the Holy Spirit. When I was a pastor, I was called upon to do many different things, but this calling is a special calling for me. If you go to someone for help in this area, you need to make sure that they know what they are talking about and that they are trained and experienced to do deliverances and exorcisms.

Different people do things in different ways, and for a deliverance to work, we meet with a client and discuss several things. First, they have to be willing to get rid of the demons. It would surprise many that some people are hesitant to get rid of demons. In fact, when it comes to certain demons, people might request that we get rid of some demons, but not all of them. That is not an option; if we are going to come in and clean out these nasty beasts, it must be all or nothing. When I was growing up, I used to take my BB gun, and I would shoot at a wasp nest. I don't recommend that because most of the time we got stung and it didn't really work out that well. Unless you kill every single one of those wasps or yellow jackets, they're going to keep coming. A demon’s nature is evil, and they may pretend to be good, but they're all evil. You have to want deliverance. We have to use discernment during an exorcism to figure out which statements are coming from the demon and which statements are from the person. Discernment is a gift from God.

It is true, and you might find this interesting, that all religions, not just Christianity, do some form of exorcism. I have found it to be true that demons even fight each other in the spirit world; they will argue with each other. We helped a young man once that had several demons.

One of the demons in him told our client to call us to get rid of his other demons, but to leave her alone. That demon spoke with a female voice. Sometimes a demon will use a person's normal voice, but sometimes they will use a voice that sounds completely different. We have heard many different voices come from the same person.

Our procedures are different than many other paranormal teams or deliverance ministries. Many times, we will engage the demons. Lots of teams and exorcists will come in immediately, praying for the demons to get out and go away. In many cases, they'll come back if you don't close the portal. We must teach, train, and disciple the individual we are working with to help them maintain their deliverance. We help them to identify and close the portals that have allowed the demons to enter or attach themselves. If they do not keep these portals closed, then there is a good chance the demons will return. These portals can be something that you know is dark and evil, but they can be something innocent. It can be a generational spirit, which is a spirit or a demon that was assigned to your family hundreds of years ago and that demon is still there. Something that we highly recommend is that if the person is not a believer in the Lord, they would accept Christ. I can assure you this makes all the difference in the world when a person is a believer, because if they are a believer then they have God's blessing. They have the power of God in them through the person of the Holy Spirit, and we can guide them through this process to use their authority in Christ.

Our prayers matter, but the client must be taught to tell the demons that they are not wanted. We guide the client to command the demons to leave in the name of Jesus Christ, and by the power of his blood. Their pathos and their passion to make these demons leave are needed. The reason that's important is because we might use our authority to make the demons leave when our team is there, but as soon as we leave, the demons will try and come back. If the person that's being delivered understands who they are and that they have the power through Christ and the ability to make the demons leave, they can conquer darkness.

We take authority over every single demon that is working in this person's life, and we bring them forth in the name of Jesus. It's kind of like when I was in law enforcement, and I would often go out and hand out subpoenas. A court ordered that you had to appear before the judge.

In a way, we do a spiritual subpoena. We order those demons, if they have had any influence on that person, if they're connected to that person, if they're attached, inside, or connected in any way, to come forward. It really gets amazing when those demons appear before us.

Sometimes we've been able to see them and have several conversations. We've spoken with them in the middle of deliverances and sometimes we feel them, but they know when we are there. I often get asked how many demons come. At times, we've had anywhere from twenty up to fifty. There have been times when there's been so many we couldn't even number them all. Incidentally, the demons do not want to come. We have to take spiritual authority over them to bring them forth, and we inquire of them why they are here and what their purposes are.

What is amazing is that out of the hundreds of exorcisms we've done, it's never been for the same exact purpose. Each demon has its own personality. Some demons work well with each other, but some demons do not. When we bind all these demons together, we make them come together, and they do not like it. They are not necessarily afraid of us, but they hate having to practice submission, submitting to the power of Christ. When we ask them questions, we inquire things of them, and we take authority. When they talk to us, there are different ways we hear them. Sometimes we hear them through the person that's there, which is not uncommon. Other times we might hear three, four, or five different voices come out of one person, and it can be male or female.

My team and I have heard audible voices in the room many times. And sometimes, when you're in the middle of an exorcism, I may hear what the demons are saying in my mind. Our team will meet after an exorcism, and one of us will say, "Did you hear the demon say this when this was happening?" And it will be word for word the same thing that they heard in their mind, showing the power of these demons. We bring those demons forth. We command them and we take authority over them, and we tell them that their dark purpose is being stopped and they're no longer going to have power in this person or situation. They are no longer going to have influence. They will no longer control how a person thinks or control their actions.

They no longer have the power to influence the person to kill themselves. Deliverances are the difference between life and death; we have done exorcism on people who have told us they would be dead today if the deliverance had not occurred.

I was a lieutenant and a chaplain for many years in law enforcement and was called to work on suicide cases. Upon arrival at the scene, I would help prepare the body for removal and work at the crime scene. I always felt a tremendously dark spirit there, and, in my opinion, I think most suicides are demonic. They are satanic, and I do not believe a person in their rational mind would commit suicide. This is not to say that every person who commits suicide is possessed. I would say they're influenced by the devil. 1 John 44 says, "Greater is he that is in me than he that is in the world." If we command the demons to leave and it's just our team commanding those demons, then what is going to keep them from coming back?

So, in the process of all deliverances, we guide the person that we are helping to also take authority over demons, and we let the person that we are delivering actually speak to those demons. This is an emotional process. These demons have often terrorized and driven people from their families. The people have been hurt by destroying relationships. This is a unique time when the person who is being attacked by these demons now takes charge. We help them talk to the demons, and many times they will say, “I can't stand you; get out of here; stay away from my children and get out of my life. You have hurt me.”

Exorcisms are long processes. Each session averages about three hours. Depending on the case, multiple sessions may be required. The demons can be weakened. Some demons may leave during the first session, but others are still requiring more deliverance. Demons act like lawyers and claim a legal right to be there. We must figure out what is giving the demon a right to be there. This is one reason it is so important for the person to be honest with us. Once we determine the source, we can guide the person to close that door. For example, they may need to renounce something that they have done. They may need to forgive someone. They may need to forgive themselves or God. It would be awesome if the demons would automatically leave and never come back, but they can be stubborn. They do not want to give up their grip on the person. It is exciting when the person now turns it around on the demons and they tell them that “I'm in charge. You’re not welcome in my life anymore.” The team and the person who is being delivered come together in unity, and we demand, we do not ask, and the authority of the demon is taken over. The demon is told they will not continue to be in this person. If we are dealing with children (which we often do), we make sure the parents are involved. The parents are there all the way through the process, and we take authority as pastors and parents. We tell the demons they have to leave. You can feel when the demons come, and you also know when they leave.

I have seen many different types of reactions during exorcisms. Sometimes the demons will try to hide, and the person will act perfectly normal at first. When we start to pray and command the demons to be exposed, there will be a reaction. At first, they may smirk at us, laugh and mock, or make fun of us. We have seen them scowl at us, and their eyes turn black. We have seen the eyes turn white. The demons may cause the person pain. The demons can be stubborn and do not want to be submissive. They may kick and yell and cuss at us. Many times, they spit up or throw up. Sometimes they will foam at the mouth. I have seen them speak in different voices. I have heard the people speak in Latin and other languages that they do not know. Sometimes they will chant. They will bring up personal information about the ministry teams' and their families that they should not know. They will threaten our families or say they will kill us before we get home. I have seen them go limp as if they are so sleepy the person cannot hear you. I have seen faces contort in very unusual ways.

In the middle of doing deliverances, the demons do everything they can to distract. The phones will ring, you can hear loud noises outside, knocking on windows, and the doorbell may ring. You may hear knocking from closets; windows and doors may slam. We have had crosses and pictures fall off the wall. We've seen levitations where people levitate in the middle of battling the demons. Levitation is where the demons take control of a person's body and lift them up into the air. People have been pushed all the way up to the ceiling, and to get them down we must take charge. The demons are ordered to bring that person down and not hurt them. Levitation is a true expression of a demonic presence. Many will ask us why they are levitating. The demons are trying to show off their power and disrupt the purpose of our being there. They want to put a spirit of fear in us. They will do everything they can to stop deliverance from happening. We have learned not to be intimidated by it.

To achieve an effective deliverance, you must respect the power of the enemy, but this does not mean you're afraid of it. You must be bold. The Bible talks about boldness, and we teach the person to have boldness through Jesus and through his power. No man can do this through their own power, and no person can get rid of these things on their own power. Working together in unity and commanding in Jesus' name is the only solution. We've seen great victories, and I have had many full deliverances, and the demons never came back.

The continued success of deliverances also depends on the person that you help. If they go back into the same lifestyle, they go back to opening portals and participate in rebellion against God or some other kind of sin, such as witchcraft. They will reopen the door to darkness, and these demons will come back. As recorded in Matthew 12, the Bible says oftentimes more of them will come back than were there originally. They'll come back with more demons, so an exorcism is not something with which to play around. You must be serious about it. We don't spend the time and resources to help unless we know a person is ready to make a change for good.

Sometimes people will fail, and they'll make a mistake, and we have to go back and do the deliverance again. We are always ready to help, and we never say no. We try and stay connected to the people that come into our lives forever. There have been times that people have fallen to temptation and the demons didn't stay away, so we needed to come back and redo the process over again. We do what we do because people need help. These demons kill and destroy people.

They keep them from accomplishing their purpose in life.

We've seen many people totally delivered from darkness. Deliverance is a process; it's not something that just magically happens. It takes work and the power of God. One thing I love about this particular ministry is when you see God win the battle. It is such a blessing. We love it when we see people that Satan has got his hand on and he's trying to destroy them, but they come to the Lord. The devil hates it when anybody gives their soul to Jesus. The Bible says whosoever calls upon the name of the Lord will be saved.

When we finish doing deliverances, we are so tired that we could lay down in the middle of the highway and go to sleep. We put everything we have into this fight, the fight between good and evil. When we do it right and under God's power with His help, we win.

*Chapter 10*

# Prayers That Defeat Darkness

## Warfare Praying that Defeats Darkness

Early in my task of helping people find freedom, God laid on my heart that we would need to gather 500 prayer warriors to pray for me and our team if we were going to have total victory in fighting demons and darkness. While my mom was living, she was the best prayer warrior for our work. When she was called to heaven, I asked the Lord, "What am I going to do without her?" The Holy Spirit quietly spoke to me, "Who told you that she was no longer praying for you?" He said boldly to me that she and the saints that have gone before us are still interceding on our behalf. He reminded me of the scripture found in Hebrews 12:1, which says, "Therefore we also, since we are surrounded by so great a cloud of witnesses, let us lay aside every weight and the sin which so easily ensnares *us,* and let us run with endurance the race that is set before us." The saints are cheering us on in battle from heaven. My mom now has a better seat from the clouds to help in the fight. I was overwhelmed and moved to tears when I understood that she is still active in helping us here on the earth.

Here's a true story from a case that happened in Corpus Christi, Texas. We were performing a full deliverance on a young woman that was possessed by several powerful demons. Our team was in a ferocious battle, which included levitation. The truth is, we lost this fight. During this intense time, we had called many prayer warriors to ask for extra prayer in the middle of the night. This was the night one of our team members was kicked hard from behind by an unseen force and left a tremendous bruise in the shape of a foot. I started praying that God would send us some heavenly help. When I served as a police officer, we had a button that we could push to get emergency help quickly. That night I wished I had an emergency button to push for immediate help!

We noticed that the woman turned and started acknowledging and speaking to some people that we could not see. She spoke out loud, "Mom, what are you doing here? You died, but you look my age." Then she said, "Grandpa, I have been missing you so much! Where is your oxygen mask?" She responded to them by admitting that she was not living a very good life and needed to stop using drugs and live a better life for Jesus. She said she knew she needed to put Jesus first in her life. She said to them, "If I do put Jesus first, how do you know that they would no longer have control over me? I want to go with you all." We could only hear one side of the conversation, but then

she said, "What do you mean it is not my time yet? I don't want to stay here." And after a moment, she said, "Okay, then I will stay and do better." We were all stunned and began to weep and quickly noticed that the demons we had been battling were gone and the room went from total darkness to a peaceful light. The young woman cried out, "My family that is in heaven came to help us fight the demons today." Our team became convinced that God had heard our prayers, and we had indeed received heavenly help from the other side to remove the demons from her life. The saints of God are fighting for us!

Now that we have established that prayer is needed in fighting against all kinds of darkness, it is important to know how to pray and what to pray in different situations.

Not all prayers are the same. When you are sick and go to the doctor, they will prescribe different medicines that can help you get well. The doctor will decide which medicine would be the most effective for the symptoms or illness. There is not just one medicine that heals all diseases or sickness. The same is true in spiritual warfare. We must be armed with different types of prayers for various situations. We must become versatile and dedicated prayer warriors.

Dr. Bill Bennett, my mentor and instructor, used to say that "If you are not praying, you are just playing." We cannot deal effectively with the demons without sincere prayer. You can do many things in your life without prayer, but let me be clear: you cannot be successful in fighting darkness without being covered in prayer.

The phrase "prayer warrior" refers to anyone who is committed to praying for others that are in need. Let me share with you three characteristics that are needed to be a true prayer warrior. They must be **focused** on the need. They must be **fervent** or passionate. They must be **fearless** and bold.

Spiritual warfare that defeats darkness is not just a simple command such as, "In Jesus' name, I command you to flee." In most cases, the situation will require a combination of prayer to God and speaking to the demons to bind them and cast them out. Our prayers are directed to God, and our warfare commands are directed to the enemy.

Start by praying for God to be with you and for the power of the Holy Spirit to give you wisdom and discernment to know the root cause of why the demons are there. A prayer of intercession could include leading the person to pray for forgiveness of their own sins and prayers to forgive those that have harmed them. The person should renounce anything in their past that could have attracted the demons or given demons the right to be there. A prayer of salvation will enable the person to have the power of the Holy Spirit to break free from Satan's bondage.

Then bind the strong man (Satan or his demons), then pray for the person.

Matthew 16:18–19 says, "And I say also unto thee, that thou art Peter, and upon this rock I will build my church; and the gates of hell shall not prevail against it. And I will give unto thee the keys of the kingdom of heaven: and whatsoever thou shalt bind on earth shall be bound in heaven: and whatsoever thou shalt loose on earth shall be loosed in heaven."

Mark 3:27 says, "No man can enter into a strong man's house, and spoil his goods, except he will first bind the strong man; and then he will spoil his house."

We have authority from Jesus to bind Satan and his cohorts. To bind evil spirits means to restrain them by addressing the demons directly and forbidding them to continue their destructive activity. We can restrict the demon's influence and power and then remove them. Through the power of the Holy Spirit, our words can free the person from the enemy's grip. We can command the demon to flee and not to return!

In prayer, we ask the Holy Spirit to minister to the person and to help them to overcome fear and failure in the future.

My goal is to give you several kinds of prayers to use when battling various kinds of demonic attacks from the devil and his demons. I want to make available to you several prayers that you can pray that will help you achieve victory. I have found that even though these prayers are simple, they are power-packed and effective. I have personally used these prayers in cases all over the nation and have found them to be extremely effective. Feel free to use these prayers as a model and modify them for your own personal situation.

Please understand that there is no lasting freedom from the devil, demons, or darkness without genuine salvation. It involves a prayer for your soul. Your soul is the most valuable thing that you own because your soul will live for eternity, either in heaven or hell. This is why both sides are fighting for it. Jesus came and died to save your soul. The devil's number one goal is to capture as many souls as he can for eternity.

I want to share with you a very clear way for you to protect your soul from Satan and to secure a place for your soul in heaven.

First of all, you must realize that you are a sinner and cannot save yourself. The Bible says in Romans 3:23 that "all have sinned and come short of the glory of God." Being a sinner means that you have done something wrong either by your actions or your thoughts. A person can even sin by not doing something that they should. If you have sinned even once, you have come short of the glory of God. This means that you are not good enough to get into heaven on your own merit or efforts. In other words, you cannot earn your way into heaven by being good or by doing good work.

Second, you must repent of your sins, which means to turn your life around to live God's way instead of living your way. It is more than just being sorry for your sin against God. It is changing to start following the Lord Jesus.

Third, you must receive the one and only Messiah Jesus, who died on the cross for all of us. To receive means to invite Jesus to come into your life to be both your Savior and your Lord. You must be willing to believe that Jesus died on the cross to pay for your sins. You must believe that after Jesus died, he came back to life on the third day.

You must be willing to commit your life to him.

Please make sure that your soul will go to heaven! You can do this by praying the following prayer or a prayer like it in your own words.

**Prayer of Salvation:**

God,

I **realize** I have sinned, and I understand that I cannot earn heaven or get into heaven because of my own efforts. Thank you for sending your son Jesus to die on the cross to pay for my sin and make it possible for me to go to heaven. I believe He died and was raised from the dead on the third day. I **repent** by turning away from my sin of rejection and all other sins and turning toward God. I **receive** the living Christ into my heart by accepting the free gift of eternal life that you have made possible for me. I accept Jesus as my Savior and as the Lord of my life. Come into my heart and save me! I **rejoice** that I will see you and other believers in heaven some day! Help me to follow you and obey you for the rest of my life.

In Jesus' name, amen.

## Prayer to Allow God to Have Control Over Your Life

This prayer is for you if you are already a Christian, but you have not allowed God to have complete control of your life. The devil certainly does not want you to give yourself over to God completely, because he knows there is power and victory in your life when you do. In Ephesians 5:17–18, it says, "Wherefore be ye not unwise, but understanding what the will of the Lord is. And be not drunk with wine, wherein is excess; but be filled with the Spirit." The phrase 'filled with' means to be controlled by God. You can pray this prayer to be filled with the mighty Holy Spirit and to let God have control over your life.

Heavenly Father,

I ask you to take all of my sins and rebellion away. Please forgive me and fill me with your Mighty Holy Spirit. I give you complete control of every area of my life. I surrender to your guidance and Lordship. Help me to understand what your will is so that I may please you. Thank you for answering this prayer.

In Jesus' name, amen.

## Prayer for Strength to Defeat the Enemy in Battle

We are told many times in the Bible that God will give us strength. God will uphold us, give us strength, and deliver us! These verses remind us that we can be overcomers and more than conquerors in the battle against evil!

Psalm 18:2 says, "The Lord is my rock and my fortress and my deliverer; My God, my strength, in whom I will trust;" Isaiah 41:10 tells us, "Fear not, for I am with you; Be not dismayed, for I am your God. I will strengthen you, yes, I will help you, I will uphold you with My righteous right hand."

I John 4:4 says, "You are of God, little children, and have overcome them, because He who is in you is greater than he who is in the world."

Here is a prayer that you can pray for strength to defeat the enemy in battle.

Almighty God,

You know my weaknesses; you are my strength! I confess to you that I am weak and tired. I know I can't fight this darkness on my own. This evil entity has been assigned to discourage and destroy me and the ones that I love. I receive the truth of the scriptures. I trust in you, God. Give me your strength. Help me to overcome the tactics of the devil. I know that you are omnipotent. You can defeat this darkness.

In Jesus' name, Amen

## Prayer for a Child Who is Under Attack

We all want to meet the needs of our children and raise them up to be happy and healthy. Our children need several things from us. They need:

Security: Children need to feel safe and not be worried about basic needs.

Scriptures: We need to teach them scripture so they will know truth and have a weapon to use in spiritual warfare.

Spankings: We need to discipline children in a loving, controlled way to teach them to be obedient and to train them up in the way they should go. Proverbs 13:24 "One who spares the rod hates his son, but one who loves him is careful to discipline him."

Support: They need not just financial support but also education support, emotional support, and most importantly, prayer support.

Psalm 127:3-4 says, *"Behold, children are a heritage from the Lord; the fruit of the womb is a reward. Like arrows in the hand of a warrior, so are the children of one's youth."*

Here is a prayer that you can pray for a Child that is under attack.

Almighty God,

I come before you on behalf of my child. I recognize that he/she is a heritage from you, a reward, and you have given them to me. I pray that you put a hedge of protection around my child. I stand in the gap for my child against all darkness and any evil agenda. Bind the demonic forces and remove them from this child. I place this child into your care. Send angels to watch over and protect this child.

Protect this child from all evil that may be attempting to penetrate their life. I claim protection and peace for this little one.

In Jesus' name, amen.

Demons,

I take authority over you. I bind you from using your influence over this child. I cast you away from this child. I command you to leave and not return. You are not welcome here! Have no more involvement in this child's life. I cover this child with the blood of Jesus.

## Prayer for Prosperity and God's Favor

There is a well-known prayer in the Bible called the Prayer of Jabez. This was his prayer.

I Chronicles 4:10 Jabez called on the God of Israel, saying, "Oh, that you would bless me indeed and enlarge my border! May your hand be with me, and may you keep me from evil, so that I may not cause pain." God granted him that which he requested.

If we pray a prayer like this one, we need to make sure that we are not being greedy or materialistic. We need to have pure motives, like being able to help others or being able to tell more people the good news about Jesus. Enlarging my border or expanding my territory could have to do with more than just land. It could mean a more influential job. It could mean improved finances so you could give more to a ministry. It could mean a bigger Bible study class to teach or a bigger group of prayer warriors with which to pray. We should also pray to be kept from evil and that we would not cause pain.

Here is a prayer for prosperity that you can pray for.

Dear God,

Please prosper me. I pray that God will bless me. Enlarge my territory. Put your hand on me and guide me. Give me wisdom and strength.

Please deliver me from all evil. Keep me from evil. Please protect me and help me to grow spiritually. Put a hedge of protection around me. Protect my finances and help me to be generous to those in need.

Help me not to cause pain to anyone. Help me be sensitive so I don't hurt people with my words or actions.

In Jesus' name, Amen.

## Pray the Lord's Prayer for Protection

Probably the most well-known prayer is called the Lord's Prayer. Jesus taught this to his disciples, and we can learn from it also. In Matthew 6:5-8, he teaches us that we should not be hypocrites or try to impress people when we pray. It is better not to just repeat prayers but to truly be sincere in praying. In the New Living Translation, verse 12 is put into words we can more easily understand: "And forgive us

our sins, as we have forgiven those who sin against us." When we look at this while considering spiritual warfare, we understand that asking for and receiving forgiveness from God can be very important to healing. Forgiving others can close a portal that has allowed demons to attach themselves to us. Finally, remember to pray for God's will and that God already knows what we need before we even ask him. The Lord's Prayer is still a great prayer for us to pray today for forgiveness and protection.

You can follow the instructions of Jesus and pray the Lord's prayer found in Matthew 6:9–13.

*Pray like this:*

"Our Father in heaven, may your name be kept holy. Let your kingdom come. Let your will be done on earth as it is in heaven. Give us today our daily bread. Forgive us our debts, as we also forgive our debtors. Bring us not into temptation but deliver us from the evil one. For yours is the Kingdom, the power, and the glory forever. Amen."

## Prayer to Close Portals and Take Back Ground That Has Been Stolen

When we are in a battle for someone, we often use the phrase, "Take back the ground that the enemy has stolen from you." This phrase comes from a story in the Bible in 1 Samuel 30. David's enemies burned his hometown and stole his family and the families of many of his men. He wept profusely then decided to go after his enemies and take back what had been stolen. With God's help, he gathered some men, and they were able to recover their land and their families. In fact, they were successful in taking back all that had been taken and more! Joel 2:25 says, "And I will restore to you the years that the locust hath eaten." Satan is a thief. John 10:10 says, "The thief does not come except to steal, and to kill, and to destroy. I have come that they may have life, and that they may have it more abundantly." Some of the things Satan can steal include our joy, our finances, our testimony, our relationships, and our health.

Here is a prayer you can pray to close portals and to take back the ground that has been stolen from you.

Lord Jesus,

In your name, I stand against Satan and his army. I know that you have promised good for me. Do not let Satan and his demons steal anything else from me and my family. Bless me and my family. I pray that everything that has been taken must be returned tenfold!

Jehovah Jireh, you are the God that provides. I pray that you will provide me with the strength and power I need to close all portals in my life. Help me to take back all the ground that the enemy has stolen. I receive all the blessings that you can and will give me. I thank you for all my past blessings and for the blessings to come in the future.

In Jesus' name, Amen

## A Prayer to Put on the Armor of God

The Bible makes it perfectly clear that we are in a battle with an enemy that we cannot see. When I was in Texas, I had the privilege of serving as a police officer. We were taught to put on our uniforms and to carry weapons to defend ourselves and others. We never went into service without first putting on our uniform and arming ourselves. There were certainly times when we would have fallen prey to the enemy if we had not been prepared. One of my law enforcement instructors told us that we had better be prepared to fight, because whether we are prepared or not, the enemy will be.

The scriptures also warn us in Ephesians 6 that we should be prepared to fight against the devil and his demons. Don't be deceived; the devil and his demons are bringing the fight to you. The scriptures found in Ephesians 6:10–17 tell us that to be strong in the Lord we should put on the armor of God.

*Finally, my brethren, be strong in the Lord and in the power of His might. Put on the whole armor of God, that you may be able to stand against the wiles of the devil. For we do not wrestle against flesh and blood, but against principalities, against powers, against the rulers of the darkness of this age, against spiritual hosts of wickedness in the heavenly places.*

*Therefore take up the whole armor of God, that you may be able to withstand in the evil day, and having done all, to stand. Stand therefore, having girded your waist with truth, having put on the breastplate of righteousness, and having shod your feet with the preparation of the gospel of peace; above all, taking the shield of faith with which you will be able to quench all the fiery darts of the wicked one. And take the helmet of salvation, and the sword of the Spirit, which is the word of God;*

Dear God,

I put on the **helmet of my salvation**. Guard my mind. Fill my mind with praise and worship for you. Give me a sound mind, and do not let me have a spirit of fear. Fill me with your Holy Spirit. Align my thoughts with your thoughts.

I put on the **breastplate of righteousness**. Forgive me my sins. I turn away from them. I renounce anything I have done that would give the demons a right to be here. Wash me white as snow. Cover me with

Jesus' righteousness by the power of the blood of Jesus Christ. Help me live a life that would please you and set a good example for others.

I put on the **belt of truth**. Jesus is the way, the truth, and the life. I trust Jesus to hold me together. Help me not to lie. Help me to only tell the truth. Help me to recognize lies from demons or people. Help me to stand firm in the truth that I am a child of God.

I put on the **gospel shoes of peace.** I stand firm and hold my ground. I will proclaim the good news of Jesus to people who need hope and peace. Help me to be sensitive to know when to share. Give me the words to say. Help me to share the good news with love and compassion.

I pick up the **shield of faith**. God protect me and my family from the evil ones. Block any fiery darts the demons may aim at me. Lead me not into temptation. Deliver me from evil. Protect me from schemes and wiles of the devil. Don't let me fall into any traps the devil has set for me. I ask that you send extra angels to help me.

I pick up the **sword of the Spirit**, which is the Word of God. I believe the Bible and claim its promises. Help me to spend time in God's word and to hide it in my heart. I know I can do all things through Christ, who strengthens me. I pray this in the powerful name of Jesus. Amen. **Prayer**

**to Break a Curse**

There are times when you feel the effect of curses. Curses can come from many places. You can be cursed by someone who is evil, like a witch or Satanist. You could be cursed by someone you know, like a family member or friend that is into darkness and is angry or has something against you. I have been told several times that a coven of witches was praying to their deity against me and cursing me.

Scripture also says you will be cursed if you curse your parents or Israel. There could be a generational curse in your family. You could be on a property that is cursed and that can affect you. You can have a self-inflicted curse from opening portals, such as using a Ouija board, tarot cards, drugs, alcohol, rebellion, or having sex with someone that has a demon.

We worked on a case in Texas where a lady went to a convention, met a man, and had sex with him. She said she felt demons come into her while they were having sex. She suffered greatly as a result. She was cursed with physical pain, and it seemed like every good thing in her life came under attack. Jeremiah 17:5 says, "Thus says the Lord: "Cursed is the man who trusts in man and makes flesh his strength, whose heart turns away from the Lord." If your heart is not turned toward the Lord, then you are not living under the protection of God's wing; therefore, you may be susceptible to a curse.

Almighty Father,

I worship you and ask for you to put a hedge of protection around me. Please help me to break free from any generational curse or curses that have been placed on me or spoken against me. I renounce anything that I may have done that has opened a portal for evil. I rebuke any curse that has been directed at me.

I claim the promise found in Isaiah 54:17, which says, "No weapon that is fashioned against you shall succeed, and you shall refute every tongue that rises against you in judgment. This is the heritage of the servants of the Lord and their vindication from me, declares the Lord." Do not let any of Satan's plans or curses succeed in hindering me or harming me in any way. I claim the heritage from the Lord instead of the heritage from my earthly family. I renounce any evil committed by my ancestors. I rebuke any generational curses and ask you to break any hold that Satan and his demons claim on my family.

I plead the blood of Jesus over every area of my life. In the name of Jesus Christ, cover me with your precious blood for protection and deliverance. Set me free from the fear and negative effects I have been experiencing. Fill me with your Holy Spirit and give me the power to be more than a conqueror in this situation. I surrender to your will for my life. Help me to be obedient and live a life that would honor you. Help me to walk in victory yet remain humble, knowing my strength and righteousness come from you. Help me remember the joy of the Lord is my strength, so I need to be faithful to spend time nurturing my relationship with you.

Break every curse that has been placed on me. 2 Thessalonians 3:3 says, "But the Lord is faithful, who shall establish you, and keep you from evil." I walk in the truth of this scripture. Keep me from evil! I give you all the glory and praise.

Amen.

## A Prayer to Overcome Fear

Isaiah 41:10 says, "Fear thou not; for I am with thee; be not dismayed; for I am thy God: I will strengthen thee; yea, I will help thee; yea, I will uphold thee with the right hand of my righteousness." We know that fear is a common human emotion. But make no mistake about it; the demons can capitalize on our fear and use it to gain a stronghold in our lives. Fear produces negative energy and allows the darkness to be present to work against us.

O God,

I know that you are not pleased with me having a spirit of fear. I know this is from the devil and from the demons. I proclaim that I am your creation and your child. I know you are watching over me. I call upon you to remove the spirit of fear and help me to eliminate fear from my life. I claim the scripture 2 Timothy 1:7 "For God hath not given us the spirit of fear, but of power, and of love, and of a sound mind." I receive this truth. Therefore, I will not walk in the spirit of fear. Give me power from the Holy Spirit to overcome all my fears.

In Jesus' name, amen.

## A Prayer to Cleanse and Dedicate Property

Sometimes property or homes need to be cleansed because darkness has claimed them. The devil and demons play the roles of lawyers and legalists. They will proclaim that they have the right to be somewhere or to be attached to someone. Demons will feel comfortable if the property has been used for satanic or new age rituals, been a burial ground, or been a place where sexual assault or other violent crimes have occurred. Suicide demons have been known to cause many people to kill themselves in the same place. In addition, we often need to cleanse property that was occupied and used by other cultures that worship nature and other gods.

Demons want to control everything on earth, including you and your property. We are told in the Bible that they want to have dominion and dominance. In a case we worked in Kansas, a home was purchased by a family who asked us to come and cleanse the home and property. They were having paranormal issues. The previous owner of the property had been sentenced to prison. He was the one I told you about, known as the skull man, and had placed over one hundred fifty human skills in the house and on the property. He was accused of holding several people in bondage on the property. We also found many other satanic symbols on the property. After a lot of work, we were able to cleanse the property. The family now lives there in total peace. They are very territorial and will often claim property, houses, or even certain items. A special thing that Telling the Truth Ministry does is conduct a worship service on the property. We claim the property for God and dedicate it for godly use.

Here is a very powerful, well-written prayer from Northwoods Church that you can pray to cleanse and bless your home and property. This is the only prayer in this book that is not written by us. I appreciate them giving us permission to share it.

Father,

Thank you for the blessing and provision of this home. Thank you for giving me authority to trample on every power of the enemy (Luke 10:19), authority to bind and loose (Matthew 16:19), and authority to release the atmosphere of heaven on earth (Matthew 6:10). Right now, in Jesus' name, I bring my home under my authority now, and under the authority of Jesus Christ. I take full authority over this home, in the name of Jesus Christ. The keys to this home have been given to me—authority has been given to me—and I take total and complete authority over this entire home now, in Jesus' name.

I renounce all ungodliness and all sinful activity that has ever taken place in this home or on this land, all the way back to Adam. I renounce the sin of all previous owners, renters, guests, and even the builder. Any curses or evil agreements ever made in or over this home I now declare broken, null, and void in the name and authority of Jesus. In the name of Jesus, I also command every foul and unclean spirit to be bound now and to leave my home. I cancel every claim and right the enemy might have here, by the blood of Jesus Christ. I cleanse this home and everything in it with the blood of Christ.

I now consecrate and dedicate this home and the land it is on to the rule of Jesus, the presence of the Holy Spirit, and the Kingdom of God. I dedicate everything in and around this house to the Lord Jesus and claim that it is under his rule, protection, and blessing—every room, all the appliances, the structure and infrastructure, the water, and the electricity.

Come, Holy Spirit. Come and fill every part of this home with the fullness of the kingdom of God, with your love, your peace, and your rest. Jesus, I ask that you would also send your angels to cleanse this home now, to establish your kingdom here, and to build a shield of protection around it. In the mighty name of Jesus Christ the Lord, I now proclaim that his home, land, and everything in it is property of the Kingdom of God.

In the powerful name of Jesus, amen.

Adapted from Eldredge, "Moving Mountains"

This prayer is used with permission from:
https://northwoods.church/book-of-prayers/cleansing-and-dedicating-property/

## A Prayer to Claim God's Authority in our Lives

Luke 10:19 says, "Behold, I give you the authority to trample on serpents and scorpions, and over all the power of the enemy, and nothing shall by any means hurt you." If you are a believer, you have been given the right to use God's name because you have been accepted into His family and His kingdom. Several years ago, one of my adopted Fox kids had an issue with her schoolteacher, and she was in trouble. She responded by saying, "My dad is Pastor Terry Fox, and I will tell him you are not being nice to me, and you will be in trouble."

The teacher called me to tell me what Trinity had said because she did not believe it was true. I had a conference with her and her teacher to work things out. Trinity knew that because she was a Fox kid, I would be there to protect her. In the same way, our heavenly Father is our protector. It is only by claiming and using God's authority that allows us to become conquerors over our enemies, the principalities of darkness and powers of evil.

Romans 8:37-39 says,"Yet in all these things we are more than conquerors through Him who loved us. For I am persuaded that neither death nor life, nor angels nor principalities nor powers, nor things present nor things to come, nor height nor depth, nor any other created thing, shall be able to separate us from the love of God, which is in Christ Jesus our Lord."

Our Heavenly Father,

We are thankful that we belong to you. Because of my personal relationship with you, I have been given the right to use your name and claim your authority over all the darkness that is coming against me. Lord Jesus, I come before you as your humble servant. I ask with all the power of the Holy Trinity that I may be able to stand firm and speak boldly against this evil that is coming against me. Fill me with your spirit and give me a sound mind so that I will have the courage to be a victorious warrior in this battle. I am thankful that you have told me that I am more than a conqueror through you.

In Jesus' precious name, amen.

## Prayer for Discernment to Know What I am Fighting and Why

It has been said that if you are going to win a battle, you need to know your enemy. Knowledge of your foe is needed to defeat the enemy. The strategy of our enemy is sometimes hidden to us. When we are out in the field helping someone with deliverance, one of the first things that our team does is to investigate who the specific enemy is and why they are being attacked. Remember, the enemy has been assigned to us and has a dark purpose in store for us.

However, the Bible tells us that we can pray and ask God for wisdom and knowledge. James 1:5 says, "If any of you lacks wisdom, let him ask of God, who gives to all liberally and without reproach, and it will be given to him."

Dear Lord Jesus,

You know all things. You created me, and you have a plan for all my days. Help me to know my enemy. Give me discernment to understand what purpose the devil has for attacking me. Expose any strongholds that there may be in my life that are allowing the demons to get a foothold. Give me knowledge and understanding. Help me not to be blinded to the truth. Help me to hear and to see the truth so I will not be confused. Holy Spirit, I ask you to help me take every thought captive so that I will only think thoughts that are pleasing to you. Open my mind so I will recognize and receive the truth and know what to do to overcome the strongholds in my life. Give me the power to act on what you have shown me to do.

In Jesus' name, Amen

## A Prayer to Overcome Strongholds

"(For the weapons of our warfare are not carnal but mighty through God to the pulling down of strong holds.) Casting down imaginations and every high thing that exalteth itself against the knowledge of God, and bringing into captivity every thought to the obedience of Christ." 2 Corinthians 10:4-5

Realize that only God in His power can remove strongholds! Our part is to yield to Him and follow His ways. God must see that we mean business. As part of breaking the bondage of a stronghold, we need to humble our souls. There are some types of strongholds that a person excuses: "Well, that's just me, and nothing can be done about it." Not so! God desires His fruit to be reproduced in every area of our lives, and the fruit of the flesh (which can become strongholds) be eliminated. Confess your sins one at a time and then forget them. God does! "If we confess our sins, He is faithful and righteous to forgive us our sins and to cleanse us from all unrighteousness." (1 John 1:9). Repent and mourn over your sin. See also James 4:9, Psalm 51:1-13, Proverbs 28:13, and Romans 8:1.

Don't rationalize your sin; just confess it. You may want to write out this confession, so when the devil (technically his demons) brings it to mind later, you can remember it has already been confessed. 1 John 1:7, 9 reminds us that when we ask for forgiveness, God removes our sin as far from us as the east is from the west (Psalm 103:12). "Let the high praises of God be in their mouth and a two-edged sword in their hand" (Psalm 149:6). Satan doesn't like to stay around praise. Negative thoughts and forces flee when we begin to praise God.

You need to ask Jesus to set you free from all negative forces associated with the stronghold. For example: inferiority, insecurity, lust, hate, guilt, etc. Command every force to leave in Jesus' name.

Satan and his forces were defeated by Christ on the cross. See Revelation 12:11; Colossians 2:13-15; Luke 10:17-19; John 17:15. Renounce, in the name of Jesus, all the forces Satan has sent against you. Renounce every activity that may have given a demon the right to oppress you. For example: playing with tarot cards or a Ouija Board, watching demonic shows or movies, rebelling against your authorities, being involved in séances, palm readings, or fortune telling, dabbling in witchcraft or the occult, getting drunk, taking drugs, listening to the wrong music, being lazy or prideful, etc. Pray and ask God to show you what the root of the sin is—where did it begin? Renounce any sin that the Lord shows you.

You will also need to make restitution when it is needed. Ask forgiveness of those you have wronged, hated, from whom you've stolen, etc. It is important to forgive all sins and hurts committed against you. You are responsible for any wrong responses you made when sinned against. Don't blame anyone else. Accept full responsibility for your responses. There is no need to detail the past, nor should you justify any of your attitudes or actions. Even if the apology is not received, God is pleased. As restitution is done prayerfully, God can do a mighty work in all persons involved.

Heavenly Father,

I come to you humbly, asking for your help to break the strongholds that Satan has in my life. Reveal to me what strongholds are in my life. I confess my sins to you now. Forgive me and cleanse me from all unrighteousness. Thank you for your faithfulness to forgive, and thank you for your cleansing power! Lord, I forgive myself and will no longer condemn and put myself down for the sins and mistakes of the past. Help me to take all negative thoughts captive. Set me free from all negative forces associated with the stronghold. I renounce in the name of Jesus all the forces Satan has sent against me. I renounce every activity I have participated in that may have given a demon the right to oppress me. I ask you to help me forgive everyone who has wronged me or hurt me in any way. Help me to control my thoughts and my actions. Help me to please you with everything that I think, say, and do!

In Jesus' name, amen.

*Chapter 11*

# Most Intense Cases

Saga of Seattle, May 29 – June 1, 2017

An Iranian pastor and his wife, Sarah, called us to come help one of their church members. He has not let them in his home for two years. He has not been to church for four years. He used to come to church regularly and even helped serve communion.

James has not left the house in about six months. He has been seeing and hearing demons talk to him. The demons are familiar spirits that appear and sound to him like people he knows. They torment him and say things that cause him to be afraid. He says they attack him with a knife, punch him, and sexually assault him. His room has knife marks in many places on the walls where he struck back at the demons and hit the walls. Although he is an adult, he begs his mother not to leave him alone with the demons. James is depressed and living in fear.

Pastor Pat Bullock, Pastor Terry Fox, and I (Barbara Fox) went to Seattle to minister to this family. The first night we were in town, we went by the house and prayed from the street. In the morning, God provided a chance meeting of a pastor and a group of his friends who prayed for us and the situation. Later that morning, we met with James' mother and brother, Mehdi. They gave us some background on James, and we find out he is very antisocial. He does not like to talk to anyone but his mother.

That afternoon, we called upon prayer warriors to be praying, and Pastor Terry and Pastor Pat went to see James. He refused to talk to them and barricaded himself in the bathroom for about seven hours. Pastor Terry spoke to him through the closed doors. James turned on the water to try to drown out his voice. Terry felt like the house needed to be blessed and turned into a house of worship. He called Pastor Massoud and his wife Sarah, and me, along with some of James' family, to come worship in the home. We sang some praise songs, sanctified the house, and then Pastor Pat shared some scripture. We anointed the house with oil and prayed over each room. Then we decided to go sing the song "Break Every Chain" upstairs by the bathroom door.

As the rest of us prayed, Pastors Terry, Pat, and Massoud all took turns talking to James, binding and rebuking the demons, and praying for James through the door. Our strategy was to be persistent and to keep wearing the demons down. The demons kept telling us to leave. At one point, the demons became very agitated, and James was hitting the walls. Pastor Terry was confronting the demon personally. The demon accused Pastor Terry of being the demon. We knew we were making progress as the demon was communicating.

Pastor Terry took authority over it. Finally, as Pastor Massoud was pleading with him to come out and let us help him get rid of the demons, God miraculously unlocked and opened the door. James was in the back of the bathroom in the tub. He pulled the curtain as the pastors went into the bathroom. When Pastor Terry opened the shower curtain, it was as if James was being pinned down. After more prayer, James came out and sat in a chair and let the pastors pray over him. He was very subdued and agreed that he knew Jesus was in him. He looked tired and defeated. It had been a seven and a half hour battle. He ate some pizza with us and came downstairs for a few minutes with us.

The next day we returned to pray with him some more. He was

much more receptive and agreed to let us pray over him willingly. He said Jesus was his friend and showed us his Bible.

We encouraged him to listen to his pastor, and let his pastor help him learn how to pray with authority.

*Chapter 12*

# Conversation with Demons

Close to the beginning of this journey in my ministry, when I was a young pastor, I went along with an older and more experienced pastor to help rid a young girl of her demons. She was a very beautiful young lady who had been selected as the winner of a statewide beauty pageant. This was over forty years ago, and I experienced one of the first conversations I had with demons. She was demon- possessed and on the verge of hurting herself and others. Her family flew us down to Texas to help try to rescue her. Upon arrival, the demons within her began to communicate with us. There were several different voices that were speaking to us through her. One of the things that one demon kept saying was, "You two don't know what you are doing."

Sometimes demons can tell the truth because they were right. I turned to the other pastor and asked him, "Do we know what we are doing?" He laughed and said, "Not really." What we did know was that God had sent us there to fight these dark and deadly forces that were in her. It is true that different ministers use different approaches when dealing with demons. Many demons seem to say the same things. After doing hundreds of cases where I have encountered demons, it makes me wonder if they have gone to school and learned talking points. In this case, the demons also said, "It is too late for you to help her." But what we did know was that, by God's grace and power, we had the authority to take on these demons and make them leave. After two hours of intense interaction, I am glad to report that every last one of these dark and dangerous demons had been removed from her.

There are three different ways that I have observed demons communicating with me. One way is that they directly speak with a nonhuman voice. Second, they have spoken to me through other people using the person's human voice. In this second case, the person is under their demonic control. Third, the most common way is that I am able to hear what they are saying in my mind. The ability to hear them in this manner is a gift and tool from God that enables me to do this ministry. Other team members who assist me have also been given this ability. Later, when we are debriefing after a case, we will learn that we all heard exactly the same messages, word for word.

When it comes to having conversations with demons, I have learned that they want to control the conversation. For instance, they do not like it when you ask them a question and demand an answer. Such as, "What name has been given to you?" For example, "How old are you?" or "Who has given you permission to be working for this person?" I do believe, as a demonologist, or even as a Christian, we have the authority to ask these questions and to demand a truthful answer. According to scripture, their nature is to lie. I believe that when we command them in Jesus' name, they must speak the truth. I have had many demons plead with me, saying, "Please do not make me answer that." Demons know that they have to show submission by answering questions. It lets them know that we are taking control of the situation. When demons declare their identity, it shows their submission.

When I was a child, if my mom or my aunt said my complete name, I knew that I was in trouble. It showed their authority. The same is true in the spirit world. There are levels of authority. In the spirit world, the ultimate authority is the Holy Spirit. I refer to him as the Mighty Spirit because, since He is part of the trinity, He is the most powerful spirit.

Demons are like lawyers. They want to debate and change the subject. They want to drive the conversation. Make no mistake about it, Satan and his army of demons like to boast and brag. When I finish with a case where I have been talking with demons, it makes me feel drained and very dirty inside and out. It is not something that I look forward to.

While working with a paranormal team in Arkansas, we were trying to purge and cleanse a house that was infested with demons. As our team was identifying what demons were there and preparing to remove them from the property, the head demon communicated to me. It said that one of the family members was molesting children in the house, and that he was the one that should have to go. It said we should make that person leave. It told me the name of the person.

After visiting with the family, we discovered that the family had filed a report of suspected child molestation already because they suspected it as well. The family was flabbergasted that we were given such personal and accurate information. Remember that demons have their own personalities and are intellectual beings. They know information and will use it to accomplish their agenda. You may wonder why a demon would give us this information. It was simply to distract us from our main purpose, which was to remove them from the property.

I would like to share with you some other interesting things that demons have said to me.

*Some things that I have heard demons say are:*

"We hate God."
"We love death."
"We love sex."

"I will share her with you. You are welcome to have sex with her."
"We wanted to kill you, but your dad would not let us."
"I am going to kill you before you get back home." This demon specifically named my hometown.
"You are a false preacher." "You are in over your head." "I will destroy your ministry."
"Your mother hates you." When I told my mom about it, she laughed. I am glad to report to you that she denied that and made it clear she did not appreciate that.
"We gave you a sore heart." I had recently discovered that I had a heart condition called atrial fibrillation. By the way, it does not slow me down.
"I am going to turn that cross upside down and stab you with it." It was referring to a cross that I use when I am doing a deliverance or exorcism.
"You will have a car wreck and die tonight." "Your plane will crash."
"You and your God are a joke."
"We have been told that we do not have to listen to you." "You are weak."
"Satan knows your name." "We will make you sick."
"We will curse you."
"See that sword on the wall? We are going to kill you with it." We were in a home in Kansas that had a large collection of swords hanging on the wall.
"Are you guys the best that God can send?" I replied back to the demon. "Then you must not be much, because God sent us here to take care of you." Which we did.
Demons often assume I am a priest and call me "Father Terry." I respond back to them and say, "No, I am Pastor Terry."
"We have dealt with you at other times."
"Get rid of those other demons, but leave me alone." "We will ruin your reputation."
"We know all your sins." I say, "Jesus knows all my sins too, and has

already forgiven me."

"You are the evil one. We are the good ones." "We know all about you."

Once I told a demon, "You are a liar." He said, "Of course I am lying. We are supposed to lie."

"She belongs to me."

"Our favorite drug is meth."

"I have been in this family for 1600 m________f_______years."

Demons

frequently cuss.

"I have killed twelve members of this family." The family did confirm the possibility that, due to strange circumstances and suicides, this could be true.

"We are not leaving."

"We have a legal right to be here."

"We have a contract with this person." "I have been exorcized before."

"Jesus should have accepted our master's offer." "Satan will rule the world."

"We fear our master, and you should!"

"When I am successful on this assignment, I will receive a promotion from my master."

"We can't die."

"Let's make a deal." "You must leave now."

"If you keep this up, we will kill her." "We own most churches."

"Atheists are fools." We have heard this several times from religious demons.

"We killed your Jesus on the cross." "Your Jesus was just a carpenter."

"Jesus was a sinner."

"We are not afraid of Jesus." However, the Bible says that they tremble at the name of Jesus.

"The resurrection didn't happen."

"We don't want to talk about the resurrection." "The resurrection is a lie."
"We know the Bible better than you." "Everyone knows the Bible is true." "The Bible is full of lies."
"Do you want to hear the Bible in Latin?"
"We are more powerful than God's angels."
"Michael the archangel is too busy to help you."
"We are from God, and he is from Satan." "If you make us leave, we will be punished." "We fear our master."
"We have two masters: Satan and God." "Heaven is not real."
"Hell is for everybody."
"Heaven is a fake place; it doesn't exist." "You will be in hell with all of us."
"Don't put us in Tartarus." Tartarus is the lowest hell, where the fallen angels were sent and are being held for judgment. It is referred to in 2 Peter 2:4 and Jude 1:6.
"I can make this person levitate."
"Do you want us to show you our power?" "Your angels can't protect you."
"We are stronger than your angel." "Your God hates you."
"If you don't stop praying right now, we will burn this house down."
"If you evict us from this person, we will destroy your family."
"We are going to make you sick."
They often call me terrible names that are cuss words.

*Things demons have said to the demonized people with whom we have been working:*

"Don't listen to him." "He is here to hurt you."
"He wants you for himself." "He is here to trick you."
"Remember how I have helped you." "I was here to help you."
"Don't make me leave. I have been with you forever." "I will make you pay if you listen to him."

“I must stay because I have been in your family for generations.” “If you make me leave, I will go to your kids.”
“We will return when he leaves.” “He doesn’t care a thing about you.”
“We will stay with you, but he will be gone.”
“Do you want me to tell him the real truth about you?”
“He is not really a preacher; he is a cop, trying to get you in trouble.”

*People have shared with us what the demons have been telling them. Here are a few of the things the demons have told people.*

“Get a Ouija board so we can communicate better.” “Have a séance so we can visit.”
“Let’s do a séance and see what happens.” “Have a tarot card reading.”
“You should enjoy magic; there is nothing wrong with it.” “Hell is not real.”
“God hates you.” “You deserve pain.”
“You should kill yourself. You are just a burden to your family.” “No one will miss you if you die.”
“I am the only one in your life that has been loyal to you.” “Your family hates you and wants you to die.”
“We can make you rich.”
“Your pastor and church hate you.”
“Don’t let these people come and remove us. We will make your life hell if you let them come.” Many times, people will cancel an appointment with us because the demons have threatened them or made them very ill.
“You are responsible for their death.” Demons try to make people feel guilty.
“We want to have sex with you. If you don’t allow us to, we will rape you.”
“God made your body for us.”

They often use the name of a deceased family member and try to convince the person that they are that dead relative or loved one. We worked a case once where the demons were texting on a phone claiming to be a dead person. There were details known that the dead person would know. The phone carrier claimed that the texts were untraceable, and that was highly unusual. The phone company could not explain where the texts came from.

We have found that demons can be both hostile and hospitable to the person at different times. They frequently try to make people think they are a friend, protector, or guide. We have seen them become very angry at the people they are attacking for asking to have them removed.

These are just a sample of some of the conversations I have heard while serving as a paranormal pastor.

*Chapter 13*

# Most Asked Questions About Paranormal

**How do you know the difference between mental illness and demonic activity?**

Mental illness is defined as a mental disorder or psychiatric disability that can cause a person to do abnormal things. Some, but not all, mental illness is caused by demons. It is our policy to encourage people who are having behavioral issues that are dangerous to themselves or others to seek psychiatric help. I prefer that people see a psychiatrist who has a Christian point of view. Many secular psychiatrists do not believe in the reality of the spirit world. However, we have received referrals from secular psychiatrists many times. We encourage people to take their medicine that has been prescribed.

Because of dealing with several hundred paranormal cases, we have found that demonic influences in a person's life can result in mental illness. They can have some of the same characteristics. It is possible for someone to have both issues. Be sure to read the chapter in this book that goes into this question in greater depth.

## Can a true Christian be possessed by a demon?

A Christian can be demonized or vexed by an unclean spirit, but not fully possessed. The definition of possession is ownership of their body and soul. God created our souls to never die. A Christian's soul belongs to God. Our soul is obviously important because Jesus died to make a way for our soul to go to heaven, and Satan wants to take our soul to hell. A believer can be demonized, which could mean they are being oppressed or influenced by a demon. To be vexed means to have a spirit influencing or harassing you. The word vexed is used more than twenty times in the Bible. A Christian can also have an unclean spirit attached to them, which would require deliverance to get rid of it.

## What should we do if we suspect a demonic attachment?

You should not ignore it. Reach out to trained professionals that can help you deal with it properly. We are here to help you determine if the problem is demonic or something else. We get lots of requests for help in determining if there is a demonic issue.

## Does a person need to be willing for the demons to be rebuked and removed?

Yes, for deliverance to be effective and lasting, the person must desire with all sincerity that the demons be removed and not allowed to come back. Otherwise, the demons will make the assumption that they are wanted and have permission to be there.

## Can a demon cause someone to commit suicide?

Yes, unfortunately they can. There are suicide demons. The enemy wants to kill people. The scripture makes this clear in John 10:10, which says, "The thief only comes to steal, kill, and destroy. I came that they may have life, and may have it abundantly." The devil wants to kill all of humanity because people have been made in the image of God. I have had many conversations with suicide demons. Some demons brag about how many people they have caused to commit suicide. Several demons have told me that when they are successful, they are promoted.

## Can a demon cause someone to write something they don't remember?

Yes, if they possess a person, they can cause that person to do things that they will not even remember. When a person is under demonic influence, a demon can cause that person to write, speak, or do things they would not normally do. Because the person is not in control of himself at the time, they may not remember saying or doing things. We have worked with people who have experienced this many times. For instance, I have had uneducated people start speaking other languages, including Latin. On many occasions, I will have talked to a demon in a person, and later, after the exorcism, the person will not remember it. However, forgetting you wrote something can also happen to people for medical reasons, such as schizophrenia or someone suffering from dementia.

## Can a demon affect electricity?

Yes, they frequently cause lights to blink and do other things to interrupt or cause fear. In the process of deliverance, we have seen the electricity go off and on frequently, and the buildings we are in sometimes shake. The reason demons do this is to show off, cause fear, or distract us. I never allow these things to distract me from the purpose at hand.

## Can a demon communicate through technology?

Yes, we have experienced this on many occasions. In one of our cases in Texas, we were asked to help a family that was receiving texts on their phone from a family member who was deceased. Demons will place unwanted pornography on people's phones or computers to tempt them. Paranormal teams sometimes use electric equipment to observe paranormal activity. We have been blessed to work with some great paranormal teams across America. In our ministry, our goal is not to go stir up or pick fights with demons, but to help deliver and rescue people who are under siege from demons.

## Can a demon move things or hide things?

Demons like to cause irritation and to hinder us from doing things that would please God. They could be trying to make you late for something or just irritate you. Demons can definitely move things. They can exert physical energy to turn pictures and crosses upside down. They can slam doors and windows. When I do exorcisms, I sometimes use a cross that has Jesus on it, which used to be owned by a Catholic priest. Demons have attacked my cross several times by knocking the Jesus emblem off it. It is not unusual for a poltergeist to move things, throw things, and frequently make noises. The term poltergeist comes from poltern, which means 'create a disturbance' and geist, which means 'ghost.' Early in my ministry, while serving as a pastor in Big Spring, Texas, a young woman in her twenties came to see me for counseling. She informed me that she had demons in her and that she could make the books fly out onto the floor. I was intrigued and asked her to show me. At that moment, some books began to move and fell over. I immediately commanded her to stop. Demons like to show off their powers when given an opportunity. I learned a valuable lesson from this. Never let demons take control of a situation.

### Can a person have more than one demon?

Yes, it is very common for people to have more than one demon. Mark 5 talks about a man who had a legion of demons. Usually there is one dominant demon that is in charge, the alpha.

### What is the difference between a ghost and a demon?

The Bible is full of extraordinary accounts of historical events. It frequently mentions demons, evil spirits, unclean spirits, and even tells of a ghost. There are 108 verses that contain the word ghost in twenty books of the Bible. In most cases it is in reference to the Holy Ghost or speaking about someone giving up the ghost, which means the person has died. A ghost is an entity that used to be alive but has died. A ghost was once a human being. A ghost is an apparition; it does not have a physical body. In Luke 24:39 Jesus says, "Behold my hands and feet, that it is myself; handle me, and see; for a spirit hath not flesh and bones, as ye see me have." Many versions of the Bible use the word ghost in this verse. Jesus is not declaring that there is no such thing as a ghost or spirit. He is saying that they do not have flesh and bones.

I personally believe in the possibilities of ghosts. There is an interesting illustration of a ghost in the Bible. I Samuel 28:3-25 gives an account of Samuel, who is dead, being summoned by a medium at the request of Saul. This account is most assuredly an unusual occurrence. This shows the possibility of a person who is dead being able to communicate with someone who is alive. However, we are warned in the Bible not to try to communicate with the dead!

Deuteronomy 18:10-12 says, "There shall not be found among you anyone who burns his son or his daughter as an offering, anyone who practices divination or tells fortunes or interprets omens, or a sorcerer or a charmer or a medium or a necromancer or one who inquires of the dead, for whoever does these things is an abomination to the Lord. And because of these abominations, the Lord your God is driving them out before you." Seeking to speak with the dead is forbidden. Remember that Satan and his demons can appear as angels of light. See 2 Corinthians 11:14. Leviticus 20:6 says, "If a person turns to mediums and necromancers, whoring after them, I will set my face against that person and will cut him off from among his people."

Demons are fallen angels. Demons can never die. Demons are much more powerful than ghosts and must be dealt with differently. There is much debate about this. Some people do not believe in ghosts at all but say they are really demons. It is true that demons will frequently disguise themselves as a loved one who has died. Demons can imitate someone who is no longer alive and can have personal knowledge.

Some people believe that it is possible for saints that have passed on to return to the earth for a short time. An example of this is that many times when a person is dying, they will see loved ones there to greet them. I would not be dogmatic on this issue.

### Is it possible to communicate with the dead? Can a medium help me contact the dead, and is it dangerous?

Yes, it is possible, but we know that we are not supposed to contact the dead. It is very dangerous because you might call forth a demon instead. I Samuel 28 contains a true story in the Bible where Saul tried to contact the dead through the witch of Endor. God did allow him to speak to a dead prophet, but the consequences were not pleasant.

Demons can pretend to be a person who is dead. They can have personal knowledge about the person's life and use that to trick people.

### What does the Bible say about communicating with the dead?

Someone who speaks to the dead is a necromancer. They are included in a list of things that God says are an abomination. Deuteronomy 18:10-12 in the King James Version says, "There shall not be found among you anyone that makes his son or his daughter to pass through the fire, or that uses divination, or an observer of times, or an enchanter, or a witch. Or a charmer, or a consulter with familiar spirits, or a wizard, or a necromancer. For all that do these things are an abomination unto the LORD: and because of these abominations the LORD thy God doth drive them out from before thee."

## What is divination? Is it a good idea to seek help from a fortune teller or medium?

According to the Merriam-Webster dictionary, divination is "the art or practice that seeks to foresee or foretell future events or discover hidden knowledge, usually by the interpretation of omens or by the aid of supernatural powers." It is not a good idea to seek guidance from a medium or fortune teller. Once my wife was talking to a woman while riding on a plane. When she found out that she was a pastor's wife, she asked for prayer. She had gone to a fortune teller, and when she left, a demon started following her. It had been following her ever since then and was causing her fear and anxiety.

## What is a necromancer?

According to the Cambridge dictionary, "a necromancer is someone who claims to communicate with the dead or who is involved in black magic." We are not supposed to seek answers from the dead. We should ask God for his wisdom and guidance instead!

## What does the Bible mean when it speaks of a familiar spirit?

The term familiar spirit is referred to several times in the Bible. A familiar spirit can be a demon that serves an individual, like a medium or necromancer. A medium can ask questions of the dead person that are personal in nature, and the demons that were around the person at the time they were alive can answer the questions. It is a deception because they are not really talking to the actual person who has died, but instead they are communicating with a familiar spirit. A familiar spirit can also be a spirit that has affected a family for generations. In one case in Kansas, a demon said that he had been assigned to that family for 1700 years. Some of the family members that were present confirmed information he was telling us about past generations.

## Is there such a thing as "good witchcraft?"

The Bible warns us against any type of witchcraft, even though some people's motives might be good. There are many forms of witchcraft. Wicca and witchcraft are very common. Witchcraft has become so popular that recently the New York Times wrote, "When did everyone become a witch?" It is estimated that in America only, there are 800,000 to a million Wiccans. This is definitely a pagan religion.

## What is Wicca?

Wicca is a modern pagan religion that originated in the United Kingdom in the 1940s. It's a nature-based belief system that emphasizes rituals and spells and is also known as "The Craft." Wiccans are polytheists who worship nature, often personified as Mother Earth and Father Sky.

## How are tarot cards and crystals used?

Tarot cards and crystals are often used together in spiritual practices to enhance intuition, provide clarity, and deepen the connection to the messages received during readings. Tarot cards are used for divination, which means seeking knowledge of the future or the unknown by supernatural means. A person doing a tarot reading may claim to offer insights into a person's past, present, and future, providing guidance on various aspects of life such as relationships, career, and personal growth. Crystals are believed to carry specific vibrational frequencies that can amplify energy and intention. They are used to enhance the intuitive and psychic abilities of the reader. Crystals can also be used to protect against negative energies and balance the energy centers in the body, known as chakras. For the record, I do not recommend using tarot cards for guidance. I do not think it is a good idea to open yourself up to being influenced by them. Dark entities could certainly be using them.

### What is Neopaganism?

Neopaganism is a modern religious movement that involves the revival of ancient pre-Christian spiritual practices and beliefs.

Neopagans may believe in pantheism, which is the worship of all gods in a pantheon, and in polytheism, which is the worship of multiple gods. They may also believe in gender equality and that there are many paths to the divine. Neopagans may worship elements of nature, such as the cycles of the moon or seasonal changes. They may also celebrate pagan observances such as the Winter Solstice, the Spring Equinox, and the Summer Solstice. Some well-known expressions of Neopaganism include Wicca, Druidism, and Germanic Neopaganism.

### How can you tell if your house is haunted? How do you know if a place is haunted?

Many people know their house is haunted because of how they feel while they are in it. Many people experience strange things that cause them to be afraid. Some people may sense they are being watched.

There could be unexplained smells, like the smell of a cigar or perfume. Many times, people end up all sleeping together in one room to feel safer. Sometimes children will be speaking or playing with someone that you cannot see. Some people's personalities may change in a house that is haunted. There can be disturbing noises and objects moving. Some people see apparitions of people or demons.

Many places are active with demonic presences due to tragic events that have happened at that property, leaving negative energy.

### Can a demon be attached to a certain place or object?

Yes, a demon may have been assigned to a certain location or attached to a certain object. We see this often in our investigations. The object could have special meaning to the demon. For instance, a lot of research shows that mirrors can be used by demons as a portal to enter a home. In some of our cases, we have encouraged people to remove objects from their home that may have attachments. Witches sometimes put curses on objects. Items that have been used in satanic rituals, idols, and statues of foreign gods should be gotten rid of. Voodoo dolls, tarot cards and Ouija boards, and crystals are other examples.

### Are Ouija Boards and Spirit Boards dangerous?

Without question, they are among some of the most dangerous tools that darkness uses to engage and entrap people. Mainstream

Christian denominations, including Catholicism, have warned against the use of Ouija boards, considering their use as Satanic practices, while other religious groups hold that they can lead to demonic possession. We have had several cases where people connected with the demon named Zozo while using the Ouija Board to communicate with the spirit world. Zozo is malevolent and has been known to cause people to commit suicide and to control people by threatening to harm their loved ones.

### Are spirit boxes and other technology equipment used by paranormal researcher's effective ways to communicate with the spirit world?

I have personally observed paranormal teams doing their investigations. I definitely believe that entities can and often do communicate through these devices.

### What are signs that someone is possessed?

This can be seen in several different ways. One of the most obvious is personality change. Extra knowledge of things they should not know could be a sign. Supernatural strength and voices telling them to hurt themselves or others are classic examples. They have a hatred toward God or people of God, such as pastors or demonologists.

### What is an exorcism? Is an exorcism biblical?

An exorcism is an attempt to evict evil spirits from a person. Scripture records that Jesus and his followers cast out many demons. The New Testament is full of accounts where unclean spirits were cast out.

Exorcisms are usually difficult and may require people that are trained to be successful. Because people frequently have more than one demon, it oftentimes takes more than one session to be completely successful. We have performed many exorcisms across America.

## Is the Catholic Church the only church that does exorcisms?

No, but they are the best known for doing exorcisms and have been successful through the years. In the Catholic Church, only certain priests authorized by their bishop are allowed to conduct an exorcism. Sadly, it may take months before they will help someone. Many Christian denominations have had successful exorcisms. Some shamans, witch doctors, psychics, geomancers, Buddhists, Islamists, Jews, Taoist priests, and Hindus also have been known to do exorcisms. In Wicca and Neopaganism, "banishing" of negativity is performed to purify an area where magic or spells are about to be performed. Both demons and angels have a hierarchy so it is possible that stronger demons can command other demons to be assigned somewhere else. As Christian exorcists, we use the power and authority that comes from God.

## Can a demon make a Christian do something?

A demon has enormous power, but it is limited in its ability to read our mind or make a believer in Christ do anything. However, he can use various kinds of temptations and strategies to influence our actions. He may have studied you, and he could know your weaknesses. Also, demons communicate with each other, so they can get information about you from other demons.

## Can a demon kill you?

Yes. Satan has death demons whose goal is to kill us. One of the main goals of demons is to kill. John 10:10 says, "The thief cometh not, but for to steal, and to kill, and to destroy: I am come that they might have life, and that they might have it more abundantly." While working a case in Van Buren, Arkansas, in the process of delivering a woman, a very dark voice came out of her saying to me, "We will kill you before you get back to Greenwood tonight." I refuted it by saying, "You do not have the permission to accomplish that." It is not unusual after working deliverance cases to have close calls while driving home. In Wichita, Kansas, we literally experienced a phantom train coming toward us on railroad tracks. We were able to avoid being struck by it, and then it faded away before our eyes. My assistant, Janie, made the statement, "I thought we were going to die!" I truly believe this was an attempt to take out our lives.

## Can a demon bother more than one person at a time?

Demons have the power to move from person to person and from location to location. They are not omnipresent like God, however. Demons and angels can only be in one place at a time. If people are in the same room, a demon could be telling them both lies and bothering them both with doubts, jealousies, causing them to question motives, etc. This is one reason it is important to put on your helmet of salvation each day, asking God to protect your mind.

## Can a demon cause people to fight or argue?

It is quite common for people to report that they fight or argue more at affected locations. They can tell lies that cause dissension.

They can cause people to have nightmares and be afraid during the night.

When people haven't had enough sleep, they can become irritable and more likely to have disagreements. Demons like to steal our joy to hurt our witness. They like to destroy marriages and relationships that help us grow closer to God.

## Can a demon-possessed person be dangerous?

A person that is possessed, under complete control of a demon, is subject to obeying the powers of darkness in them. While serving in law enforcement, I dealt with a lady who had just drowned one of her children. I asked her why she did it. She replied that God told her to kill the child. She told me it was difficult to do because he really fought her. This is another reason I hate Satan. In reality, it was Satan guiding her to do this horrible deed. On many occasions, while doing a deliverance with someone, the person will tell me that they are hearing voices telling them to kill me and my team. A person that is possessed by demons can also display inhuman strength. There is lots of documentation to support this. It is not unusual for them to kick or hit. Once while I was a young pastor in Corpus Christi, Texas, a mother brought her twelve-year-old son to me to pray over him. She said he was possessed. When I started to pray over him, he became violent and physically attacked his mother with tremendous force. He tried to strangle her to death. With my law enforcement background and experience, I should have been able to restrain him with no problem. However, this was not the case. In my attempt to restrain him, my office took a beating. Furniture was overturned. I put out a call for emergency assistance from other police officers. Upon their arrival, they were astonished also by his strength. One of the officers said, "This kid must have the devil in him."

### Are the things I see about paranormal activity on TV and in the movies true?

Obviously, some things you see in media are sensationalized or exaggerated. For example, the *Ghostbuster* movies make fun of the spirit world. I personally think it is unwise to joke around about paranormal issues because it causes people not to take it seriously. Some paranormal teams that you see on TV are not legitimate. They could manipulate things to happen for their shows. I have been blessed in my paranormal ministry to work with some paranormal teams that are very skilled and have integrity. They use their skills to help people. Many of the things you see on the movies and television can be true. Often the producers of movies are demonically inspired, and sometimes they are biblically accurate. This stuff is real. For example, the 2023 movie *Nefarious* showed how a demon could control someone in a biblical and realistic way.

### What is the difference between a cult and the occult?

As a pastor, I can provide some insights into the differences between a cult and the occult.

A cult is a group or movement that is often centered around a charismatic leader or a set of beliefs that are considered outside of mainstream society. Cults typically have controlling and manipulative practices that can be harmful to their members. They may isolate members from friends and family, exhibit extreme devotion to the leader, and often have a closed belief system that is not open to questioning. Cults can have religious, spiritual, or even secular ideologies. A church or denomination can be a cult if they do not believe in biblical doctrines such as the trinity.

The occult, on the other hand, refers to practices, beliefs, and phenomena that are beyond the scope of normal human understanding. This can include dark practices related to magic, divination, and astrology, and would include the use of tarot cards, crystals, Ouija boards, and participating in witchcraft. The occult is often associated with hidden or secret knowledge that is not readily apparent or understood by the general public. Often times people in the occult have altars dedicated to deities that are false gods or demons. Satanic rituals can sometimes include animal sacrifices and human sacrifices.

It's important to note that while both cults and the occult can involve beliefs and practices that are outside of mainstream religions, they are distinct in their focus and nature. Cults are more about social dynamics and control, while the occult is more about hidden knowledge and dark practices.

### Can animals be possessed? Can pets be possessed?

Yes, in fact there is a story in the Bible where Jesus cast some demons into some pigs. Then the pigs ran off the cliff and were killed. Demons can occupy living things and can control them and use them.

### Could my pet be sensing evil spirits even though I can't see anything?

Yes, frequently pets will resist entering a certain room or hallway if they sense something. Sometimes they will growl or hiss at something that we cannot see. We should pay attention to them. Animals have the ability to sense and hear things more than humans. Some breeds of animals have echolocation abilities. We did a case once where the dogs had been shut in a room and became so terrified that they clawed the wood of the door to pieces to get out.

## Are prayer walks biblical?

Yes, we can take the light of God into all darkness. We can apply God's authority over God's creation. Our team has had positive experiences on prayer walks in Bakersfield, California. Many people have asked us to come back because they can see the difference that it can make. In the Bible, it says that we are to pray without ceasing, so prayer walks are definitely biblical.

# Letters of Affirmation

**Letter from Reverend Pat Bullock:**

As a fellow pastor in Texas and a Director of Missions for the Heart of Kansas Southern Baptist Association, it has been my privilege to serve the Lord alongside Pastor Terry Fox for thirty-five years. He was raised by a praying single mom in Greenwood, Arkansas, who invested many hours in diligent prayer for God to be glorified in his ministry.

He and I have traveled the world together. We served on the International Mission Board for many years. He was chairman of the Southeast Asia Committee, and I served as chairman of the Overseas Committee. We had the privilege to see our Southern Baptist missionaries sharing the gospel in a number of countries overseas.

Terry also served on the North American Mission Board as chairman of the board of trustees. His vision was to start churches everywhere possible in America. His passion is to see people come to know Christ as Savior. His call is to lead people to receive Jesus as Lord and Master. He is called to be involved in the paranormal ministry with the ultimate goal to see people set free and see them saved. I have had the opportunity to see Pastor Terry's effectiveness while ministering to people struggling with paranormal issues. He gives God the glory when he experiences the victory of seeing people delivered from darkness in this specialized ministry. He can be trusted to put people's needs and concerns above his own interests. His goal is to glorify Christ and see believers live a victorious life in the love of Jesus. I believe God has gifted him to deal with paranormal encounters with an authority that comes from the Holy Spirit.

I believe Terry has authored this book to help shed light on this very important subject. He endeavors to bring glory to Christ and to point to the truth that Jesus is the sovereign Lord of all creation, both in the spiritual realm and the physical realm.

**Letter from Steven Jenson:**

Many things in our lives are measured by the circumstances that we go through. Much like measuring things from before my 30th birthday and after my 30th birthday. Meeting brother Terry Fox in 1984 at Gardendale Baptist Church was one of those moments. I have considered it an honor and a privilege to know him and call him my friend and my Christian brother since that time.

We've been through a lot together. He has witnessed me fall and get lifted back up by the Lord, and I have seen him do the same. At the time we met, I was working with the Nueces County Sheriff's Department and was involved in a minor accident. My lieutenant, Guy Genovese, knew of my relationship with Terry Fox and contacted him. Terry had not had much interaction with me until that time, other than being my pastor. He dropped what he was doing, as I would learn later was his way. He came to the hospital where I was and visited with and prayed for me for several hours. After that, we became close friends. We were viewed in the community as best friends.

A short while later, he shared with me his interest in police work. It had been in his heart for years to serve the world in that way. I invited him on several ride-alongs with me, which he gladly accepted and enthusiastically showed up for. After going on several ride- alongs, we approached the sheriff and asked about having Brother Terry as the chaplain for our department. The sheriff was more than willing to have Terry serve as the chaplain, as he was a pastor of a large Baptist church in the area and was well respected in the community.

Terry began to serve in this capacity and later got more and more involved with law enforcement on the street. It was not long before Terry went to the academy and graduated and became a full Deputy Sheriff. I can recall several occasions with my brother Terry, and I worked well into the late-night hours Saturday and early Sunday morning hours until about 5 AM. We would go home clean up, meet for some breakfast, and then head to the church by about 7:30 on Sunday morning. There we would pray together, and Brother Terry would fine-tune his sermon for the morning. I was always amazed at how he could stand up and preach the word of God so strongly and showed no signs of having been up all night with me, in the bars chasing the bad guys.

I was assigned as a detective in the missing persons and child protection unit. Of course, Terry followed me there and was very excited to be a part of that team. Our Lieutenant also embraced Brother Terry as a respected deputy and leader in the community. It was not long until the 1990's brought on a large influx of what we called "devil worshipers" at the time. We found many occasions where there were signs of devil worship. On one occasion, Brother Terry had invited, as he always did, a young girl, who was probably about 16 years old, to come to church. To his surprise, she showed up. He had promised her that there would be no one there that she knew and no one there who would hurt her or know anything about her past. I was unaware of her visit and attended church on Sunday morning, like every other Sunday.

The girl approached Terry after seeing me and asked, "What is he doing here? I don't want him here! I hate him! Some people want to kill him." Terry calmed her down and prayed with her; he talked to her and assured her that I was not the bad guy and that we were there to help her. She continued coming to church and eventually was saved by our Lord. Terry was the reason for her salvation. I have no idea where she is today, but I'm sure wherever she is, she has a memory of Terry, me, the Sheriff's Department, and most importantly, our Lord and Savior.

Many twists and turns have come through the lives of my brother, Terry, and myself. Divorce, remarriage, friendships, and moves to other states apart from one another. But I always have brother Terry in my heart, and I know he has me in his heart. There is no separation of what God brings together. I will always be honored to know him and work with him, but mostly to call him a friend, and I still call him my pastor. Brother Terry has become involved in battling demons, not something I have the nerve or strength to do. I am impressed with the many stories he has shared with me about flushing demons out of people, out of people's homes, and out of people's lives. But most importantly, after flushing out the devil, those people have come to know the Lord and rejoiced in their salvation. That's the most important thing I can say about Terry Fox: wherever he is, wherever he goes, whatever ministry he is in, be it police work or Christian work, he always leads people to the Lord.